ALAN BENNETT

A Life Like Other People's

ff

faber and faber

P

PROFILE BOOKS

First published in 2005 in *Untold Stories*
This edition first published in 2009
by Faber and Faber Ltd
Bloomsbury House, 74–77 Great Russell Street,
London WC1B 3DA

and

Profile Books Ltd
3A Exmouth House
Pine Street, Exmouth Market
London EC1R 0JH
This paperback edition first published in 2010

Typeset by Faber and Faber Ltd
Printed in CPI Bookmarque, Croydon, Surrey

A CIP record for this book
is available from the British Library

ISBN 978–0–571–24813–1

2 4 6 8 10 9 7 5 3 1

There is a wood, the canal, the river, and above the river the railway and the road. It's the first proper country that you get to as you come north out of Leeds, and going home on the train I pass the place quite often. Only these days I look. I've been passing the place for years without looking because I didn't know it was a place; that anything had happened there to make it a place, let alone a place that had something to do with me. Below the wood the water is deep and dark and sometimes there's a boy fishing or a couple walking a dog. I suppose it's a beauty spot now. It probably was then.

'Has there been any other mental illness in your family?' Mr Parr's pen hovers over the Yes/No box on the form and my father, who is letting me answer the questions, looks down at his trilby and says nothing.

'No,' I say confidently, and Dad turns the trilby in his hands.

'Anyway,' says Mr Parr kindly but with what the three of us know is more tact than truth, 'depression isn't really mental illness. I see it all the time.'

Mr Parr sees it all the time because he is the Mental Health Welfare Officer for the Craven district, and late this September evening in 1966 Dad and I are sitting in his bare linoleum-floored office above Settle police station while he takes a history of my mother.

'So there's never been anything like this before?'

'No,' I say, and without doubt or hesitation. After all, I'm the educated one in the family. I've been to Oxford. If there had been 'anything like this' I should have known about it. 'No, there's never been anything like this.'

'Well,' Dad says, and the information is meant for me as much as for Mr Parr, 'she did have something once. Just before we were married.' And he looks at me apologetically. 'Only it was nerves more. It wasn't like this.'

The 'this' that it wasn't like was a change in my mother's personality that had come about with startling suddenness. Over a matter of weeks she had lost all her fun and vitality, turning fretful and apprehensive and inaccessible to reason or reassurance. As the days passed the mood deepened, bringing with it fantasy and delusion; the house was watched, my father made to speak in a whisper because there was someone on the landing, and the lavatory (always central to Mam's scheme of things) was being monitored every time it was flushed. She started to sleep with her handbag under her pillow as if she were in a strange and dangerous hotel, and finally one night she fled the house in her nightgown, and Dad found her wandering in the street, whence she could only be fetched back into the house after some resistance.

Occurring in Leeds, where they had always lived, conduct like this might just have got by unnoticed, but the onset of the depression coincided with my parents' retirement to a village in the Dales, a place so small and close-knit that such bizarre behaviour could not be hidden. Indeed it was partly the knowledge that they were about to leave the relative anonymity of the city for a small community where 'folks knew all your business' and that she would henceforth be socially much more visible than she was used to ('I'm the centrepiece here') that might have brought on the depression in the first place. Or so Mr Parr is saying.

Mam and Dad in the back garden, 1966

My parents had always wanted to be in the country and have a garden. Living in Leeds all his life Dad looked back on the childhood holidays he had spent holidays on a farm at Bielby in the East Riding as a lost paradise. The village they were moving to was very pretty, too pretty for Mam in her depressed mood: 'You'll see,' she said, 'we'll be inundated with folk visiting.'

The cottage faced onto the village street but had a long garden at the back, and it seemed like the place they had always dreamed of. This was in 1966. A few years later I wrote a television play, *Sunset Across the Bay*, in which a retired couple not unlike my parents leave Leeds to go and live in Morecambe. As the coach hits the M62, bearing them away to a new life, the wife calls out, 'Bye bye, mucky Leeds!' And so it had seemed. Now Dad was being told that it was this longed-for escape that had brought down this crushing visitation on his wife. Not surprisingly he would not believe it.

In their last weeks in Leeds Dad had put Mam's low spirits down to the stress of the impending upheaval. Once the move had been accomplished, though, the depression persisted so now he fell back on the state of the house, blaming its bare unfurnished rooms, still with all the decorating to be done.

'Your Mam'll be better when we've got the place straight,' he said. 'She can't do with it being all upset.' So, while she sat fearfully on a hard chair in the passage, he got down to the decorating.

My brother, who had come up from Bristol to help with the move, also thought the state of the house was to blame, fastening particularly on an item that seemed to be top of her list of complaints, the absence of stair-carpet. I think I knew then that stair-carpet was only the beginning of it, and indeed when my brother galvanised a local firm into supplying and fitting the carpet in a couple of days Mam seemed scarcely to notice, the clouds did not lift, and in due course my brother went back to Bristol and I to London.

Over the next ten years this came to be the pattern. The onset of a bout of depression would fetch us home for a while, but when no immediate recovery was forthcoming we would take ourselves off again while Dad was left to cope. Or to care, as the phrase is nowadays. Dad was the carer. We cared, of course, but we still had lives to lead: Dad was retired – he had all the time in the world to care.

'The doctor has put her on tablets,' Dad said over the phone, 'only they don't seem to be doing the trick.' Tablets seldom did, even when one saw what was coming and caught it early. The onset of depression would find her sitting on unaccustomed chairs – the cork stool in the bathroom, the hard chair in the hall that was just there for ornament and where no one ever sat, its only occupant the occasional umbrella. She would perch in the passage, dumb with misery and apprehension, motioning me not

to go into the empty living room because there was someone there.

'You won't tell anybody?' she whispered.

'Tell anybody what?'

'Tell them what I've done.'

'You haven't done anything.'

'But you won't tell them?'

'Mam!' I said, exasperated, but she put her hand to my
mouth, pointed at the living-room door and then wrote
TALKING in wavering letters on a pad, mutely shaking her
head.

As time went on these futile discussions would become
less intimate (less caring even), the topography quite spread
out, with the parties not even in adjoining rooms. Dad
would be sitting by the living-room fire while Mam hovered tearfully in the doorway of the pantry, the kitchen in
between empty.

'Come in the pantry, Dad,' she'd call.

'What for? What do I want in the pantry?'

'They can see you.'

'How can they see me? There's nobody here.'

'There is, only you don't know. Come in here.'

It didn't take much of this before Dad lapsed into a weary silence.

'Oh, whish't,' he'd say, 'be quiet.'

A play could begin like this, I used to think – with a man on stage, sporadically angry with a woman off stage, his bursts of baffled invective gradually subsiding into an obstinate silence. Resistant to the off-stage entreaties, he continues to ignore her until his persistent refusal to respond gradually tempts the woman into view.

Or set in the kitchen, the empty room between them, no one on stage at all, just the voices off. And what happens when they do come on stage? Violence, probably.

It was all so banal. Missionary for her sunless world, my mother was concerned to convince us in the face of all vehement denial that sooner or later she would be taken away. And of course she was right.

Her other fears . . . of being spied on, listened to, shamed and detected . . . were ordinary stuff too. This was not the territory of grand delusion, her fears not decked out in the showy accoutrements of fashionable neurosis. None of Freud's patients hovered at pantry doors; Freud's *selected* patients, I always felt, the ordinary not getting past, or even to, the first consultation because too dull, the final disillusion to have fled across the border into unreason only to find you are as mundane mad as you ever were sane.

Certainly in all her excursions into unreality Mam remained the shy, unassuming woman she had always been, none of her fantasies extravagant, her claims, however irrational they might be, always modest. She might be ill, disturbed, mad even, but she still knew her place.

It may be objected that madness did not come into it; that, as Mr Parr had said, this was depression and a very different thing. But though we clung to this assurance, it was hard not to think these delusions mad and the tenacity with which she held to them, defended them, insisted on them the very essence of unreason. While it was perhaps naïve of us to expect her to recognise she was ill, or that standing stock still on the landing by the hour together was not normal behaviour, it was this determination to convert you to her way of thinking that made her behaviour hardest to bear.

'I wouldn't care,' Dad said, 'but she tries to get me on the same game.' Not perceiving her irrationalities as symptoms, my father had no other remedy than common sense.

'You're imagining stuff,' he would say, flinging wide the wardrobe door. 'Where is he? Show me!'

The non-revelation of the phantom intruder ought, it seemed to Dad, to dent Mam's conviction, persuade her that she was mistaken. But not a bit of it. Putting her finger to her lips (the man in the wardrobe now having mysteriously migrated to the bathroom), she drew him to the window to point at the fishman's van, looking at him in fearful certainty, even triumph; he must surely see that the fate she feared, whatever it was, must soon engulf them both.

But few nights passed uninterrupted, and Dad would wake to find the place beside him empty, Mam scrabbling at the lock of the outside door or standing by the bedroom window looking out at a car in the car park that she said was watching the house.

How he put up with it all I never asked, but it was always this missionary side to her depression, the aggressiveness of her despair and her conviction that hers was the true view of the world that was the breaking point with me and which, if I were alone with her, would fetch me to the brink of violence. I once nearly dragged her out of the house to confront an elderly hiker who was sitting on the wall opposite, eating his sandwiches. He would have been startled to have been required to confirm to a distraught middle-aged man and his weeping mother that his shorts and sandals were not some subtle disguise, that he was not in reality an agent of . . . what? Mam never specified. But I would have seemed the mad one and the brute. Once I took her by the shoulders and shook her so hard it must have hurt her, but she scarcely seemed to mind. It just confirmed to her how insane the world had become.

'We used to be such pals,' she'd say to me, shaking her head and refusing to say more because the radio was listening, instead creeping upstairs to the cold bedroom to perch on one of the flimsy bedroom chairs, beckoning me to stay silent and do the same as if this were a satisfactory way to spend the morning.

And yet, as the doctor and everybody else kept saying, depression was not madness. It would lift. Light would return. But when? The young, sympathetic doctor from the local practice could not say. The senior partner whom we had at first consulted was a distinguished-looking figure, silver-haired, loud-talking, a Rotarian and pillar of the community. Unsurprisingly he was also a pull your socks up merchant and did not hold with depression. At his happiest going down potholes to assist stricken cavers, he was less adept at getting patients out of their more inaccessible holes.

How long such depressions lasted no doctor was prepared to say, nor anyone else that I talked to. There seemed to be no timetable, this want of a timetable almost a definition of the disease. It might be months (the optimistic view), but one of the books I looked into talked about years, though what all the authorities did seem agreed on was that, treated or not, depression cleared up in time. One school of thought held that time was of the essence, and that the depression should be allowed to run its course unalleviated and unaccelerated by drugs. But on my mother drugs seemed to have no effect anyway, and if the depression were to run its course and it did take years, many months even, what would happen to my father?

Alone in the house, knowing no one in the village well enough to call on them for help, he was both nurse and gaoler. Coaxing his weeping parody of a wife to eat, with every mouthful a struggle, then smuggling himself out of the house to do some hasty shopping, hoping that she would not come running down the street after him, he spent every day and every fitful night besieged by Mam's persistent assaults on reality, foiling her attempts to switch off the television, turn off the lights or pull the curtains against her imaginary enemies, knowing that if he once let her out of his sight she would be scrabbling at the lock of the front door trying to flee this house which was both her prison and her refuge.

Thus it was that after six weeks of what Dad called 'this flaming carry-on' it was as much for his sake as for hers that the doctor arranged that she should be voluntarily admitted to the mental hospital in Lancaster.

Lancaster Moor Hospital is not a welcoming institution. It was built at the beginning of the nineteenth century as the County Asylum and Workhouse, and seen from the M6 it has always looked to me like a gaunt grey penitentiary. Like Dickens's Coketown, the gaol might have been the infirmary and the infirmary the gaol. It was a relief, therefore, to find the psychiatric wing where Mam was to be admitted not part of the main complex but a villa, Ridge Lee, set in its own grounds, and as we left Mam with a nurse in the entrance hall that September morning it seemed almost cheerful. Dad was not uncheerful too, relieved that now at any rate something was going to be done and that 'she's in professional hands'. Even Mam seemed resigned to it, and though she had never been in hospital in her life she let us kiss her goodbye and leave without protest.

It was actually only to be goodbye for a few hours, as visiting times were from seven to eight and though it was a fifty-mile round trip from home Dad was insistent that we would return that same evening, his conscientiousness in this first instance setting the pattern for the hundreds of hospital visits he was to make over the next eight years, with never a single one missed and agitated if he was likely to be even five minutes late.

I had reached early middle age with next to no experience of mental illness. At Oxford there had been undergraduates who had had nervous breakdowns, though I never quite believed in them and had never visited the Warneford Hospital on the outskirts of the city where they were usually consigned. Later, teaching at Magdalen, I had had a pupil, an irritating, distracted boy who would arrive two hours late for tutorials or ignore them altogether, and when he did turn up with an essay it would be sixty or seventy pages long. When I complained about him in pretty unfeeling terms one of the Fellows took me on one side and explained kindly that he was 'unbalanced', something that had never occurred to me though it was hard to miss. Part of me probably still thought of neurosis as somehow 'put on', a way of making oneself interesting – the reason why when I was younger I thought of myself as slightly neurotic.

When I was seventeen I had had a friend a few years older than me who, I realise when I look back, must have been schizophrenic. He had several times gone through the dreadful ordeal of insulin-induced comas that were the fashionable treatment then, but I never asked him about it, partly out of embarrassment but also because I was culpably incurious. Going into the army and then to university, I lost touch with him, and it was only in 1966, on the verge of leaving Leeds, that I learned that he had committed suicide.

I went to the funeral at St Michael's, Headingley, the church where in our teens we had both been enthusiastic worshippers. Every Friday night a group of us gathered in the chancel to say the office of Compline with, at the heart of it, Psalm 91: 'Thou shalt not be afraid for any terror by night: nor for the arrow that flieth by day. A thousand shall fall beside thee,' we sang, 'and ten thousand at thy right hand: but it shall not come nigh thee.' Now it had, and as the remnants of our group stood awkwardly outside the church, I reflected that he was the first person of our generation to have died. Oddly it was my mother who was most upset, far more so than her acquaintance with him warranted, the fact that he had not died a natural death but had committed suicide seeming particularly to grieve her in a way I might have thought strange were not her own shadows by that time already beginning to gather.

Driving over the moors to the hospital that evening, I thought how precarious our previous well-being had been, how unwittingly blessed in our collective balance of mind, and how much I'd taken it for granted. I said so to Dad, who just stared out of the window saying nothing. Sanity and its vagaries were much discussed at this time, the fashionable theorists R. D. Laing and Thomas Szasz. Their ideas had never impinged on my father nor were they likely to; balance of mind was something you were entitled to take for granted so far as he was concerned, 'Item no. 1 on the agenda, to get your Mam back to normal.'

Except affliction was normal too, and this one seemingly more common than I'd thought. Arriving at the lighted villa in its own little park, we found we were far from alone, the car park full, the nurse busy at Reception, and hanging about the entrance hall, as in all institutions (hospitals, law courts, passport offices), characters who joked with the staff, were clued up on the routine and, whether visitors or patients, seemed utterly at home. It was one of these knowing individuals, a young man familiar rather than affable, who took us along to what the nurse said was Mam's ward.

He flung open the door on Bedlam, a scene of unimagined wretchedness. What hit you first was the noise. The hospitals I had been in previously were calm and unhurried; voices were hushed; sickness, during visiting hours at least, went hand in hand with decorum. Not here. Crammed with wild and distracted women, lying or lurching about in all the wanton disarray of a Hogarth print, it was a place of terrible tumult. Some of the grey-gowned wild-eyed creatures were weeping, others shouting, while one demented wretch shrieked at short and regular intervals like some tropical bird. Almost worse was a big dull-eyed woman who sat bolt upright on her bed, oblivious to the surrounding tumult, as silent and unmoving as a stone deity.

Obviously, I thought, we have strayed into the wrong ward, much as Elizabeth Taylor did in the film of *Suddenly Last Summer*. Mam was not ill like this. She had nothing to do with the distracted creature who sat by the nearest bed, her gown hitched high above her knees, banging her spoon on a tray. But as I turned to go I saw that Dad was walking on down the ward.

We had left Mam at the hospital that morning looking, even after weeks of illness, not much different from her usual self: weeping and distraught, it's true, but still plump and pretty, clutching her everlasting handbag and still somehow managing to face the world. As I followed my father down the ward I wondered why we were bothering: there was no such person here.

He stopped at the bed of a sad, shrunken woman with wild hair, who cringed back against the pillows.

'Here's your Mam,' he said.

And of course it was only that, by one of the casual cruelties that routine inflicts, she had on admission been bathed, her hair washed and left uncombed and uncurled, so that now it stood out round her head in a mad halo, this straightaway drafting her into the ranks of the demented. Yet the change was so dramatic, the obliteration of her usual self so utter and complete, that to restore her even to an appearance of normality now seemed beyond hope. She was mad because she looked mad.

Dad sat down by the bed and took her hand.

'What have you done to me, Walt?' she said.

'Nay, Lil,' he said, and kissed her hand. 'Nay, love.'

And in the kissing and the naming my parents were revealed stripped of all defence. Because they seldom kissed, and though they were the tenderest and most self-sufficient couple, I had never seen my father do anything so intimate as to kiss my mother's hand and seldom since childhood heard them call each other by name. 'Mam' and 'Dad' was what my brother and I called them and what they called each other, their names kept for best. Or worst.

They had been Lil and Walt in their courting days, living on opposite sides of Tong Road in the twenties. Marriage and children had changed them to Mam and Dad, and it took a catastrophe for them to christen themselves again.

So when in 1946 he collapsed in the street and was taken to St James's with a perforated ulcer, Dad became Walt once more. And when Mam was crying with pain having had all her teeth out, she was not Mam but Lil. And to him she was Lil now

There was only one chair by Mam's bed and no room for another; besides, Mam was crying, and Dad too, so I walked round the ward. Though many of the patients were unvisited, their disturbance and distress unalleviated by company, other beds hosted families as stunned and bewildered as we were. They sat huddled round a stricken mother, or a weeping daughter, careful to avoid the eye of other visitors and with none of the convivialities and camaraderie a usual hospital visit engenders.

Yet there were others who seemed entirely at ease in these surroundings, elderly sons of vacant mothers, jovial husbands of demented wives, and some whose faces were more coarse and void than those of whom they were visiting. They sat round the bed in bovine indifference, chatting across the demented creature in their midst, as if the lunacy of a loved one was no more than was to be expected.

It was from this time I conceived a dislike of Lancaster

I've never since lost. Having seen madness on that ward, I saw it echoed in face after face in the town. Though it's a pleasant enough place I find the people there less amiable and appealing than elsewhere in Lancashire, with the possible exception of Liverpool. There's an openness and generosity in Blackburn, Preston and Rochdale, maybe because these were virtues fostered in the mills; Lancaster, commercial, agricultural and (like Liverpool) once a port, seems sullen, tight-fisted and at night raw and violent.

Sometime in the course of this terrible hour a neat middle-aged woman stopped at the foot of Mam's bed.

'It's Mary, love. I'm off now. They've just rung me a taxi.' She turned to me. 'Could you just go and see if it's come?'

I went out into the entrance hall, cheered that one of these desperate women could, by a stay even in such unpromising surroundings, be recovered for normality and turned back into a sane and sensible creature. There must after all be hope. But if there was hope there was certainly no taxi, so I went back to the ward. Mary had by now passed on, making her farewells at another bed. I went over to tell her the taxi hadn't come only to find she was now telling her tale to an empty pillow.

In her ensuing bouts of depression Mam was in three hospitals and in each one there was a Mary, a Goodbye Girl who hung about the door, often with her bag packed, accosting everyone who came in, claiming she was about to leave, with the taxi ordered.

'Are you my taxi?' she would say to anyone who came near, though this persistent expectation of departure did not necessarily mean she was dissatisfied with her circumstances, and there are after all worse ways to live than in a constant readiness to depart. The irony was that it would only be when she stopped thinking that she was on the point of departing that she would be pronounced cured and allowed to do so.

The next night I got into conversation with a pleasant young man who was sitting in the entrance hall and whom I took to be a student, possibly at Lancaster University. He was telling me in great detail about a forthcoming visit to Russia and I asked him how he was planning to go.

'By Ribble Motors. They run a coach service to Moscow starting every night from Morecambe Pier.'

If these were lighter moments they hardly seemed so then. A nurse told us that this was the Admissions Ward where, until diagnosis could sort them out, the confused and the senile, the deranged and the merely depressed were lumped together for observation, the implication being that the next ward would be better. It could hardly be worse, and to leave Mam in such a situation a moment longer than we had to seemed unthinkable. I longed to bundle her up then and there and, as in some Dickensian deliverance, convey her far away from this yelling hell-hole to a place that was light and calm and clean.

After two days' obstruction by the ward sister we eventually managed to see the doctor in charge, who was kindly and understanding but as weary and defeated as someone out of Chekhov. He would be happy, he said, to have her transferred to another hospital if we could arrange it. I cannot think nowadays it would be so easy, and there would be the rigmarole of quotas to be considered and competing budgets, but in those days it just meant a visit to the Mental Health Welfare Officer, and it is this errand that has brought us straight from Lancaster to Settle this September night, to Mr Parr's bleak office above the police station.

'Nearly done,' says Mr Parr. 'What did Mrs Bennett's parents die of?'

'Her mother died of cancer,' I say, 'and her father had a heart attack.' Dad shakes his head, meaning that these questions seem to him to have little to do with Mam's current illness. At least that's what I take him to mean and I reckon not to see, because while I tend to agree I don't think now is the time to make an issue of it.

As Mr Parr is noting this down Dad gently touches my knee. This is a man who never touches, seldom kisses, but Oxford-educated as I am and regularly to be seen on television I fail to appreciate the magnitude of the gesture, and blunder on.

'Well, perhaps not a heart attack,' I say. 'It may have been a coronary thrombosis. He dropped dead anyway.'

It was in 1925, in the kitchen at Gilpin Place, the spot pointed out: there by the dresser your Grandad died, plain in the sight of everybody. That they were not living at Gilpin Place at the time never, of course, occurred to me.

The form completed, Mr Parr locks up his office, walks us back along the street to where we have parked the car; he promises to make the arrangements for Mam's transfer the next day, and we say goodnight.

'Did those questions matter?' asks Dad. 'Would they

affect the treatment?' I tell him that I don't think so and that what Mr Parr was after, presumably, was whether there had been anything similar in the family before. I start the car. 'Only it was your Grandad Peel. He didn't have a heart attack. He killed himself.'

I turn the engine off, sit there and digest this, Dad volunteering no more information. Eventually, though it doesn't seem to me to affect Mam's situation one way or another, I go and knock on Mr Parr's door and explain that I'd just this minute found out that Mam's father didn't die of a heart attack; he had drowned himself in the canal.

Mr Parr doesn't think it's relevant either, but standing on his doorstep as we drive away he may well be thinking that this is an odd family that censors its own history, and it's that that's relevant.

As we drove home Dad told me that as soon as the interview started he realised the true facts of Mam's father's death were likely to come out, and it was this that had made him want to put his hand on my knee, lest the suicide be a shock. It had been a shock, but the shocking thing was not the act itself so much as the way it had been concealed and misrepresented for more than forty years.

Truth to tell I found the suicide intriguing too (and felt ashamed a little that I did so). Like a child who longs to be an orphan, or at least not the offspring of his humdrum parents, I was excited by this man who had drowned and had his drowning buried; it made my family more interesting. In 1966 I had just begun to write but had already given up on my own background because the material seemed so thin. This perked things up a bit.

In fairness to myself I had never known my grandfather, nor understandably in the circumstances had he been much talked about. 'He was a lovely feller' was Mam's description of him, her stock phrase for men she liked; his only son, her brother Clarence, was a 'lovely feller' too, killed at Ypres in 1917, and when his time came my father would also be a 'lovely feller'. 'Your Grandad Peel', as he was known to distinguish him from 'Your Grandad Bennett', occurred in some of the family photographs I used to find in the dresser drawer at Grandma's where I went rooting as a child. He was a stocky man with thick dark hair and a moustache, not fierce-looking

Grandad Peel

as some of the men in old photographs were but with no clue as to what he was like. Mam had said he was keen on 'nature study' and knew about trees and flowers; he went on walks.

The drowning, though, straightaway shed light on an incident early in her depression which at the time I'd thought almost a joke. Dad had gone out and Mam and I were alone in the house. Motioning me into the passage where we would not be overheard, she whispered that she had done something terrible. I was having none of it, but she got hold of my arm and pulled me up the stairs and pointed to the bathroom but would not go in. There were six inches of water in the bath.

Mam and Gordon with Aunty Kathleen

My mother's family, the Peels, had once been well-to-do, owning mills in Halifax, and were descendants, so Mam's sister Myra claimed, of Sir Robert Peel. The youngest of the three sisters, Aunty Myra was the keeper of the family flame, determined that if her present did not amount to much, a sales assistant in White's Ladies' Mantles Shop in Briggate, now living in a back-to-back in Wortley, then the past could be called in to compensate. When my brother was christened, Aunty Myra wanted him given Peel as a middle name, and there was a muttered row at the font when Dad, who thought one name sufficient and two pretentious, would have none of it. He didn't have much time for the Sir Robert Peel business either, or with any attempt to put it on or talk posh, which Aunty Kathleen and Aunty Myra both went in for. But even my mother, who took his line, thought that the family had come down in the world, saying that there had been two branches of the Peels in Halifax, both with mills, and that at the time of the Boer War the run on cloth for uniforms had tempted their branch of the family, her grandfather possibly, to invest in new machinery. With the end of the war came a slump and with it bankruptcy, the other less enterprising branch of the family going on to further prosperity. Certainly every Christmas on the mantelpiece of the back-to-back in Gilpin Place there would be a grand card from some country Peels, whom I took to be the gentry they had become and we might have been. But it may all have been romance; in private life Beatrice Lillie was Lady Peel and my aunties even adduced her as a distant connection.

The mill gone, my grandparents then bought a hardware shop in West Vale outside Halifax but that too went bankrupt, through sheer kind-heartedness my mother said, and letting too much stuff out on credit. There is a picture of the shop in the sheaf of crumpled photographs and newspaper clippings that passes for our family album, the shop assistants lined up on the steps flanked by those Karnak columns of linoleum that enfiladed every hardware store even in my own childhood, and peeping through the door my mother's blurred ten-year-old face.

The shame of this second bankruptcy drove the family to Leeds, where they lived in Wortley, Grandad Peel now managing a gents' outfitters in Wellington Road. The three sisters, Kathleen, Lilian and Lemira, and their elder brother

Clarence all went to Green Lane School, its gaunt hulk one of the few buildings undemolished among the new houses dinky as houses in Monopoly that nowadays cover the slopes below Armley Gaol; the school, the gaol and St Bartholomew's Church all that is left of a thriving neighbourhood, the pillars of a sometime community.

All this I sort of knew in 1966 but without ever enquiring into the details, our family history a series of vivid scenes of uncertain chronology and mostly connected with Mam's side of the family. There was Uncle Clarence's death at Ypres and the telegraph boy riding his bike along Bruce Street in 1917, with women stood fearfully on their doorsteps to see which door he would knock at. There was Mam, working upstairs at Stylo Shoes in Briggate in 1926, watching mounted police charge the strikers. There was the outbreak of war, the actual declaration catching us on a tram going down to Vicar Lane bus station to get a bus to safety and Pateley Bridge; VE night outside Guildford Town Hall, sitting on my Uncle George's shoulders, marvelling at floodlights, which I'd never seen before. And Grandma Peel sitting in her chair at Gilpin Place in 1949, beginning to bleed from the womb, and as Aunty Kathleen cleans her up joking grimly, 'Nay, lass, I'm seventy-nine but I think I must be starting again.'

Still, if I knew little of my mother's family I knew even less about my father's, not that there seemed much to know. My father was not a typical butcher – thin, anxious, dogged all his life by stomach ulcers and a temperament ill suited to the job. The youngest of four brothers, he had lost his mother at the age of five, when his father, faced with bringing up four sons, had hurriedly remarried. This second wife was a narrow, vicious woman, a stepmother out of a fairy story; she was pious, chapel-going and a hypocrite who beat the youngest boys, Walter and George, and then told lies about them to her new husband so that when he came home from work he gave them the strap again. Whereas the elder boys were old enough to escape the house and too big to beat, Dad and his brother George ('our butt' as he always called him) bore the brunt of her frustrated rage. It was she who put him to butchering at the age of eleven, an offence for which he never forgave her but which earned her her nickname. To this day I don't know what she was really called, and I have never troubled to find out, but she was always referred to by all the Bennetts as the Gimmer, a gim-

My father, aged twelve

mer a sheep that has no lambs and a nickname Dad must have brought home from the slaughterhouse in Oldfield Lane, where he was condemned to work. I can only just remember her, a figure in shiny black satin seemingly out of the depths of the nineteenth century but who must have died in the early forties. Shortly before her death she immortalised herself in the family by saying to my nine-year-old brother, Gordon, 'Get off that stool, you, or I'll kick you off.' Her funeral was an occasion of undiluted joy, sheer hysteria breaking out among the mourners when her coffin went down into the grave and Mam slipped and nearly went after it.

Grandad Bennett was as bald as an egg. He had worked at the gasworks in Wellington Road, the stench of which pervaded the acres of sooty red-brick streets around Armley Gaol. He had been in an explosion which perhaps literally or as the result of shock blew away all his hair, a cruel fate in our family, where the men all have thick and often un-greying hair. His second wife's piety must have infected him because in his old age he took to marching behind the Salvation Army band, his gleaming head jeered at by the unfeeling youths of Lower Wortley.

At some point when he was still a boy Dad took it into his head to learn the violin. Why he chose an instrument that in its initial stages is so unrewarding I don't know; it's one of the many questions I never got round to asking him. He got no help at home, where he could only practise in the freezing parlour, the Gimmer too mean even to let him have any light so that he had to manage with what there was from the gas lamp in the street outside. Whether he was born with perfect pitch I don't know but in later life he would play along to the hymns on the wireless, telling you the notes of the tune he was accompanying as easily as if he was spelling a word. In happier circumstances he would have been a professional violinist but there was never any hope of that and a butcher he remained, working firstly for the Co-op, before in 1946 buying a shop of his own, which he had to give up ten years later through ill health, then buying a smaller one and the same thing happening. With no money to speak of and the job having given him precious little satisfaction, he was never so happy as when in 1966 he was able to give up butchering for good.

Happy, that is, until 'this business with your Mam'. Driving backwards and forwards to Lancaster, I had never spent so much time with my father as then, and though there was no other revelation as startling as that to do with Grandad Peel, he talked more freely than he'd ever done about Mam and their life together, the car a kind of confessional. I was doing the driving and it helped that road safety precluded much eye contact, my own occasional embarrassment betrayed by abrupt bursts of speed as I suddenly put my foot down as if to get away as fast as I could from the past he was talking about.

The suicide, though, he could not be persuaded to discuss. Having let on to the fact, he still seemed to want to keep it hidden and would not be questioned about it, sensing perhaps that my interest in it was as drama and only one stage up from gossip. As a child I was clever and knew it, and when I showed off, as I often did, Dad would not trouble to hide his distaste. I detected a whiff of that still; he was probably wishing he'd kept his mouth shut and never mentioned the tragedy at all.

I did ask about his other revelation, 'the similar do' he had told Mr Parr that Mam had had just before they were married. Had that been to do with the suicide, I asked, as it must have been around the same time? Not really, said Dad. He thought it was more to do with their wedding.

It had never occurred to me as a child that there were no photographs of my parents' wedding. Along with the cut-glass fruit bowl, the stand of cork table mats and the lady leashing in her Alsatian, a wedding photograph was a component of the sideboard of every house of every friend or relative that I had been into. Typical was the wedding photograph of Uncle George and Aunty Flo, taken around 1925. Uncle George is in a suit, wing collar and spats, Aunty Flo in a white wedding-dress and veil, the folds of her dress carefully arranged to cascade down the sooty steps of St Mary of Bethany, Tong Road, where Uncle George sings in the choir, and watched off-camera by their respective families, the Rostrons and the Bennetts, and also by anybody who happens to be waiting this Saturday morning at the tram stop at the bottom of Fourteenth Avenue.

The absence of a similar photograph from our sideboard had never struck me. And if it was not on the sideboard nor was it in the top right-hand dressing-table drawer in Mam and Dad's bedroom where, along with a pot of wintergreen ointment and an old scent spray and the tuning fork for Dad's violin, the family photographic archive was kept. It was a slender collection, fitting easily into two or three tattered Kodak wallets and consisting chiefly of snaps of holidays at Morecambe or Filey: Mam stroking a baby donkey on the sands somewhere, Dad in a bathing costume holding Gordon up to the camera, the pair of us, me a baby, Gordon three, sitting on Grandma's knee on the wall at Gilpin Place. But no wedding.

At the seaside: Mam with Uncle George and Auntie Flo

The natural assumption by an imaginative child, particularly if he was a romancer as I was, would be that he was illegitimate or at any rate not his parents' child. Both possibilities had occurred to me, but I had seen their marriage certificate (also kept in the dressing-table drawer) and this disposed of the first possibility while a look in the mirror put paid to the second. There, depressingly, was the same pink face and long chin that all the Bennetts had. Grandma would sometimes take me with her when she went bowling at the Recreation Ground, her friends (black cloche hats, long duster coats) would look at me in the pushchair and say, 'Oh yes, Poll. He's a right Bennett.' It was never something I much wanted to be, until a year or two ago, unexpectedly coming across my cousin Geoff in a hotel car park in Wetherby, I saw both his father, Uncle George, in his face and my father too, and the grin neither of them was ever able quite to suppress, and I was not unhappy that I looked a bit like that too.

Had I given any thought to the missing photographs I would probably have taken this to be just another instance of our family never managing to be like other families, of which there were far more urgent and contentious instances than a mere unrecorded ceremony. There was never being allowed to wear an open-necked shirt, for instance, for fear we caught TB; there was never going without a cap lest we got sunstroke; never having a drink of cold water and it always having to be 'aired', and not being allowed to share a lemonade bottle with other boys (TB again), after Wolf Cubs most of my friends would have two-pennyworth of chips, but we weren't supposed to as they kept us awake, Mam even smelling our breath for vinegar just in case. Our family was no better or worse off than our neighbours but in all sorts of ways, that were no less weighty for being trivial, we never managed to be quite the same.

On the other hand, had there been a photograph of Mam and Dad's wedding it was likely to have been an early casualty of Mam's precocious interest in antiques, which led to a gradual purge of items like the fruit bowl, the table mats and the woodpecker calendar. Wedding presents though these items often were, the forties saw them gradually relegated to the attic to be replaced by her first tentative acquisitions from junk shops: a brass candlestick she bought in Ripon for 8s. 6d.; a green glass doorstop; a chipped lustre jug. To her credit she had never gone in for the lady and the Alsatian dog or (worse) the little boy holding a smockful of cherries who often kept her company. Both these items were unhesitatingly dubbed as 'common' by my mother, and she would be mortified today to see them on bric-à-brac stalls enjoying equal status with the lustre and the candlesticks, one as much sought after as the other, collectables all.

There was no question that Mam's liking for these ancient *objets trouvés* was entirely genuine, though in acquiring them she was also laying claim to a sort of refinement which was genuine too; it was hard to say where it came from, women's magazines, possibly and in particular Beverley Nichols's column in *Woman's Own*. Some of it, though, was instinctive if not inbred. She knew, for instance, without having read it anywhere, that the old-fashioned kitchen range that we had was preferable, had more 'character' than the tiled fireplaces everybody round about thought were the height of sophistication, and that the brass pot which held our fire irons was superior to the ceramic knight-in-armour wielding poker and tongs that stood sentinel on neighbouring hearthstones.

Desperate I think it now, and touching too, this faith she

had in what constituted a better life. It couldn't be called a hobby, it was never systematic enough for that, though going through cupboards at home nowadays I'll still sometimes come across one of the many little notebooks she started, with wispy drawings of chair-backs labelled 'Sheraton' or 'Hepplewhite', and lists of pottery marks she copied out of library books; then there are some blank pages and another list, 'Bits of music I like': Chopin's Polonaise in A, Mendelssohn's *Italian Symphony*, *The Dream of Olwen*, the spelling all over the place.

Nowadays when 'bygones' are the stuff of half a dozen TV programmes, and nuggets of the more tuneful classics are trotted out to the banalities of disc jockeys who can scarcely pronounce the composers' names, such aspirations in a middle-aged working-class woman would not be particularly remarkable. But in Leeds in 1946 it was precocious if not eccentric, particularly since it hardly linked up with the way we lived, over a butcher's shop in a house with no hallway, the living room giving straight onto the street where Mam's painfully collected gentilities were periodically overwhelmed by the stench of fat being rendered in the cellar. Nothing she bought was ever worth much, her

Staffordshire ornaments were always cracked, the 'Shera-ton' chair an Edwardian reproduction and the turbanned Rockingham man smoking a pipe had lost his hand (a little mitten-like paw made of plasticine Mam's unconvincing prosthesis).

Still, her antiques, touching though they were in their inadequacy, were not an attempt to improve our social status. Though she herself would have said she liked 'old stuff' because it was 'classy', this definition had nothing to do with class, 'classy' in her vocabulary simply the opposite of 'common'. That was the real nub of it. Because if there was one consideration that determined my parents' conduct and defined their position in the world it was not to be (or to be thought) common.

Common, like camp (with which it shares a frontier), is not easy to define. At its simplest meaning vulgar or ostentatious, it is a more subtle and various disparagement than that or was in our family anyway, taking in such widely disparate manifestations as tattoos, red paint, yellow gloves and two-tone cardigans, all entries in a catalogue of disapproval that ranged through fake leopard-skin coats and dyed (blonde) hair to slacks, cocktail cabinets, the aforementioned ladies with Alsatian dogs and boy with cherries, and umpteen other embellishments, domestic and personal.

The opposite of 'common' is not 'uncommon'; indeed an element of uncommonness in the ostentatious sense is part of being common – the dyed blonde hair and leopard-skin coat of Miss Fairey, the chemist's assistant at Armley Moor Top, or twenty years later the white Jaguar in which Russell Harty's parents would roll up to visit him in Oxford. So flaunting it (whatever 'it' was) and splashing money around were part of it. But so was having no aspirations at all or living in something approaching squalor while squandering money on gambling or drink; that was common too.

A dog could be common – a barbered poodle – but seldom a cat; colours like the red of paint (on a house) and purple (practically anywhere). 'Them's common curtains,' Mam's frequent observation from the top deck of a bus; it always had to be the top because Dad was a smoker and it served as a grandstand for a running commentary on the social scene. 'Tangerine! I wouldn't have tangerine curtains if you paid me. And look at that camel-hair coat. Makes him look like a bookie.' Haircuts were a dangerous area: if Dad had his cut too short he was thought to look 'right common'; cafés, too, particularly those doing too much fried stuff but omitting to serve toasted teacakes. These days shell suits would undoubtedly be condemned, as would walking down the street drinking from a can, and it would do as a definition of what's gone wrong with England in the last twenty years that it's got more common.

Such fastidious deprecations were invariably made privately and to each other, my parents too timid to think their views worth broadcasting or that they might be shared with anyone else, still less meet with general agreement; this reticence helping to reinforce the notion that we were a peculiar family and somehow set apart. Cheerful, rumbustious even within the security of the home, off their home ground they were shy and easily intimidated; there was an absence of swagger and they never, unlike my mother's self-confident sisters, 'had a lot off'. So when they stigmatised ostentatious behaviour as common it reaffirmed their natural preference not to want to attract attention and to get by unnoticed; they knew what they took to be their place, and kept to it.

Wanting to go unnoticed was what Mam's depression was about. Pressed to define why it was she found the village intimidating, she said, 'You don't understand. I'm the centrepiece here.' So it was hardly surprising that when Dad revealed that there had been something similar in the past it should have been on the eve of her wedding, an occasion when there could be no going unnoticed either: 'I'm the centrepiece here', which is a bride's boast, was my mother's dread. Was this why there were no photographs?

What was agitating her, and maybe it agitated him too, as he was in many ways more shy even than her, was the ceremony itself and the churchful of people it would inevitably involve. Marriage is a kind of going public, and I could see, as Dad couldn't or wouldn't, that coming to live in the village which had maybe brought on this second bout forty years later was a kind of going public too.

Not that the ceremony she was dreading was likely to be an elaborate one, as neither family can have had any money. A proper wedding, though, would have run to bridesmaids and they were there to hand in her two sisters, Kathleen and Myra, and this may well have been part of the trouble, as she had always felt overshadowed by them and something of a Cinderella. Unlike her they revelled in any kind of public show, edging into whatever limelight was going. Later in life they made far more of my brother's and my achievements than Mam and Dad did. When I got my degree at Oxford Dad wrote, 'We haven't let on to your aunties yet that you're getting your cap and gown. You won't be wanting a lot of splother' – splother Dad's word for the preening and fuss invariably attendant on the presence of the aunties.

The splother attendant upon the wedding was harder to get round, and Mam's fear of the occasion persisted until there came a point, Dad told me, when they nearly broke off their engagement because neither of them could see a way of ever getting over this first necessary hurdle. Eventually Dad sought the advice of the local vicar.

These days this would mean a cosy, even chummy chat with counselling the keynote. And why not? But Leeds in those days was the proving ground for many a future dean or bishop, some of the grandest Anglican dynasties – Hollises, Bickersteths, Vaughans – ministering to the slums of Hunslet and Holbeck. St Bartholomew's was a great slum parish too, its huge black church set on a hill above Armley and Wortley, and though the slums around it have gone, or at any rate changed their character, its heavy spire still dominates the south-western approaches to Leeds. The

St Bartholomew's Church, Armley

vicar in 1928 was the Reverend H. Lovell Clarke, subsequently Archdeacon of Leeds, and it was to him rather than to one of his several curates that Dad went.

It must have been hard to explain: all brides are nervous, after all; why should this Lilian Peel require special treatment? Public school and Cambridge, the vicar is just the kind of figure ('very better class') to make Dad nervous and tongue-tied. What he has come along to ask is whether the vicar will marry them at seven-thirty in the morning, with no fuss, no congregation and in time for Dad to get to work at Lower Wortley Co-op by eight-fifteen. Lovell Clarke says that this is out of the question; the law does not permit him to marry anyone before eight in the morning. However, he has no objection to performing the ceremony beginning at eight o'clock, and surely if he is getting married the Co-op won't mind if he is half an hour late for work? Dad enquires: the Co-op does mind; he has to be at work by eight-fifteen.

There are occasions in life, often not in the least momentous, which nail one's colours to the mast. There was the morning, ten days before the end of my National Service, when a sergeant in the Intelligence Corps at Maresfield made me scrub out a urinal with my bare hands; another when a consultant at the Radcliffe Infirmary discussed my naked body without reference to me with a class of smirking medical students; and though it occurred years before I was born, this moment in St Bartholomew's Vicarage when my father, baffled at every turn, tells Mr Lovell Clarke that he cannot get a quarter of an hour off work in order to get married is another. Logic, education, upbringing leave such moments unshifted and unforgotten. They are the self at its core.

My father, I suspect, gives up at this point but the vicar does not, and indeed comes up with a solution that is ingenious,

My parents, shortly before they were married

even cheeky. To begin with the young couple will need a special licence from the Bishop of Ripon, dispensing with the need for the banns to be read, the vicar sensibly assuming that whatever plan he comes up with is better carried out quickly rather than waiting the three weeks that proclaiming the banns will involve. Then armed with the licence they are to present themselves at the church at seven-thirty the following morning, at which time the vicar will say the whole wedding service up to but not including the vows, thus complying with the law. On the stroke of eight the vows themselves can be said, the ring put on and this young butcher still have time to get to work by eight-fifteen. And on 28 September 1928 that is how it is done. Dad goes off of work, Mam goes home and in the evening, in lieu of a honeymoon, they get tickets for the Theatre Royal to see *The Desert Song*.

That was why there was no photograph on top of the sideboard or in the dressing-table drawer. At eight o'clock on a sooty September morning it would have been too dark; besides, a photograph would have taken time and would in any case have probably come under Dad's definition of 'splother'. But were I a poet I would write about those moments in that great empty church, the anxious groom in his working clothes with his tentative bride, and the urbane cleric, standing on the altar steps waiting for the clock to strike, the pause before the off. A former chaplain to nearby Armley Gaol, where prisoners used regularly to be hanged, Lovell Clarke must have waited many times for eight o'clock, the pause before a more terrible off. What he was like I have no idea, though I imagine him as a clergyman of the old school. But across seventy and more years, Herbert Lovell Clarke, I would like to shake your hand.

In every other circumstance a man who hung back, follower not leader, visiting his wife in hospital my father was always in the front rank. The second the visiting bell went he would hurry down the ward ahead of the rest of the pack, always with a carrier or a parcel containing the vest he had washed or some of the Creamline toffees Mam liked and a few marigolds from the garden. And though he might have come thirty miles he was always on the dot, no second of the permitted time let go to waste.

Ferrying him to the hospital at Lancaster those first few nights I found his insistent punctuality irritating, particularly as there seemed to me nothing to be punctual *for*, so much of the visit passed in silence with Dad just sitting by the bed holding Mam's hand. They seemed even in misery such a self-contained couple that I thought he would have been happier coming alone. Their absorption in each other was total and almost wordless, a kind of anxious courting, and feeling spare I'd leave them to it, and wandering about the hospital or trailing glumly round the perimeter I reflected that to have a mother who is deranged is bad enough, but that wasn't really why I was there; I was there because, alone among my contemporaries, I had a father who couldn't drive.

He had made at least two attempts. Twenty years before, in the late forties when he had had his first shop, he had invested in a second-hand motorbike and sidecar; except that it wasn't a sidecar but a large coffin-like box which Dad, never happier than when he had a brush in his hand, straightaway painted green. The theory was that Dad would go round on this dilapidated combination delivering orders to his customers in Far Headingley, Cookridge and West Park. And perhaps this did happen once or twice, though since delivering necessarily involved a good deal of stopping and starting, and starting was not the bike's strong point, this mode of transport never became a regular routine or superseded the push-bike with its basket (*W. Bennett, High Class Meat Purveyors*) pedalled laboriously up the suburban drives and crescents of north Leeds by 'The Boy'.

I suspect the motorbike was bought as another means of escape, something to 'go off' on at weekends perhaps or for little evening runs round the lanes of Adel, Eccup and Arthington. It's hard to imagine, looking back, that Mam could ever have been persuaded to ride pillion, but though she was never keen ('too draughty for me') she was still

Dad in the Otley Road shop

game enough in those days to give it a try. Had crash helmets been obligatory then, that would have clinched it, as I cannot imagine either of them got up in the necessary gear. As it was, Mam would be in her usual clothes ('my little swagger coat and that turban thing') and Dad in his raincoat and trilby, making any concessions to what this mode of transport required thought by them to be pretending to be something they weren't . . . and they certainly weren't bikers. Sometimes even all four of us would go out, with Gordon

Otley Road, 1950

and me laid on a bit of old curtain inside the closed box.

Dad had never got as far as a test and still had L-plates, and though helmets might not be obligatory it was already an offence for a learner driver to carry passengers. Thus it was that on one of our few outings as a whole family the bike was flagged down by a particularly pompous local policeman, PC Brownlow, who proceeded to lecture Dad on this point of law; Mam presumably still sitting on the pillion clutching her eternal handbag, mortified at this public humiliation, particularly in a part as better class as Adel.

His lecture on the Highway Code completed, PC Brownlow lengthily puts away his pencil and adjusts his cape so that my brother and I, thinking he's gone, choose this moment to open the lid of the box and reveal our presence, thus triggering a further lecture. Dad is ordered to drive home alone as Mam and my brother and I trail back to the tram terminus at Lawnswood, all of us knowing that the bike's days are now numbered.

Though it straightaway took its place on the list of 'your Dad's crazes' (fretwork, fishing, home-made beer) the idea of a motorbike wasn't instantly extinguished, dwindling away via another short-lived investment in a contraption called a Cyclemaster, whereby a motor was attached to the back wheel of a pedal cycle, and which came into play when climbing hills. Or didn't, as proved too often to be the case, so that it ended up like the fretsaw and the double bass advertised in the Miscellaneous Column of the *Yorkshire Evening Post*. After this they stuck to the bus.

It wasn't until twenty years later, when Dad was over sixty and they knew they were about to leave Leeds, that

Dad had some driving lessons and took his test in Harrogate. Always a considerate man, he had got it into his head that courtesy towards other drivers was on a par with the more basic requirements of the Highway Code. The result was that coming up to one of the town's many elaborately planted roundabouts he was so concerned to raise his hand to another driver who had given way to him (out of prudence, I should think) that he drove the wrong way round the Floral Clock and was failed instantly.

Harrogate had always been a favourite place with my parents, but the recollection of this humiliation was so keen that they seldom went there again and when he did take some more driving lessons it was in Skipton and he kept it a secret. The night of his test he telephoned me in London, but boasting was so foreign to him it was some time before he mentioned it. 'I took your Mam out in the car this afternoon.' 'Oh, that's nice,' I said, not catching the reference. 'I thought we'd have a run out. I passed my test.' For him it was as if he had joined the human race. Nothing that he had ever accomplished gave him so much pleasure or, I think, made him feel so much a man.

His first and only car was a khaki-coloured Mini which

transformed their lives, put paid to hanging about in bus stations and set them free to range the countryside and visit places they had only read about. It affected my life, too, though in ways which, for them, were less welcome. Previously I had gone north at regular intervals really to chauffeur them around and give them a change of scene. Now I stayed longer and longer in London and saw them much less.

It meant, too, that when Dad rang to say 'I think your Mam's starting another depression do', there was not the same urgency to hurry home. He did not need me to ferry him the fifty miles round trip to the hospital. Now he could manage on his own, and manage he did, though Mam was often in hospital five or six weeks at a time. This was at Airedale, near Keighley, further than Lancaster it's true but modern and with better facilities. He drove there every day with no thought that he could do anything else, and in due course it was his conscientiousness and devotion to duty that killed him.

Love apart, what led my father to drive fifty miles a day to visit his wife in hospital was the conviction that no one knew her as he knew her, that if she were to regain the shore of sanity he must be there waiting for her; finding him she would find herself.

Years later I put this in my only play about madness, with Queen Charlotte as devoted to her husband, George III, as ever Dad was to Mam.

'It is the same with all the doctors,' the Queen says. 'None of them knows him. He is not himself. So how can they restore him to his proper self, not knowing what that self is.'

How could any doctor, seeing this wretched weeping

Wilsill, Nidderdale, *c.*1940

woman, know that ordinarily she was loving and funny and full of life? Dad knew and felt that when she woke from this terrible dream he must be there to welcome her and assure her that she had found herself.

So together they trailed the long system-built corridors of the hospital, empty on those August afternoons – summer always her worst time; they sat by the unweeded flower beds, watched the comings and goings in the car park, had a cup of tea from the flask he had brought and a piece of the cake he had made. 'I think she's beginning to come round a bit,' he'd say on the phone. 'They say next week I can take her for a little run.'

The hospital where she was most often a patient was one of those designed by John Poulson, the corrupt architect who made his fortune in the sixties by deals done with city bosses all over the north. Architecturally undistinguished and structurally unsound – it was said to be slowly sliding down the hill – the hospital was still streets ahead of the ex-workhouse at Lancaster or the old St James's in Leeds, where Dad himself had all but died. 'Well, if Mr Poulson did one good thing in his life,' Dad would say when Mam was on the up and up, 'it was this hospital. It's a grand place.'

And featureless though it was, it was indeed light, airy, cheerful and split up into small manageable units. The snag was that these units, colour-coded though they were, were all more or less identical. Even for those in their right minds this could be confusing, but for the patients who were already confused, like those on the psychiatric ward, it was doubly disorienting. Psychiatric was not far from Maternity, with the result that the unbalanced would wander into what looked to be their ward only to find what they took to be their bed was now occupied by, as Mam said, 'one of these gymslip mums. She didn't look more than fourteen,' her language and her humour discovered intact where she had abandoned them months before. 'She cracked out laughing this afternoon,' Dad said. 'They're going to let her come home for the weekend.'

Early on in her first bout of depression and not long after she had been transferred from Lancaster Moor to a smaller and less intimidating institution near Burley in Wharfedale, Mam was given electro-convulsive therapy. We had no thought then that ECT was particularly invasive, an interference with the mental make-up or a rearrangement of the personality, and I do not think this now more than thirty years later, when ECT is even more controversial and to some extent discredited. I do not, then or now, see it as torture or punishment and no more routinely decreed or callously administered than any other treatment, though these were the objections to it at the time as they are the objections to it now. So far as my mother is concerned, she does not show any alarm at the prospect, and talks about the procedure with curiosity but without apprehension.

This was the period when the fashionable analyst was R. D. Laing and madness, while not quite the mode, was certainly seen as an alternative view of things, the mad the truly sane a crude view of it. In practical terms (though it was never practical) enlightenment consisted in encouraging the mentally ill to work through their depression, schizophrenia or whatever to achieve a new balance and an enhanced sense of self; the most extreme case and often-quoted exemplar being Mary Barnes, who came to a revised perception of herself via a period in which she smeared the walls in excrement. I thought at the time that this was not on the cards for the average patient or for the unfortunate nurse or relative who eventually had to clean up after them, though this didn't seem to enter into the equation.

I had a similar difference of sympathy about the same time when at the long-gone Academy Cinema in Oxford Street I saw Ken Loach's film *Family Life*. It's about mental illness and includes a scene in which a doctor prescribes ECT for a patient, at which point the audience in the cinema roundly hissed the supposed villain. Unable to join in or share the general indignation, I felt rather out of it. Faced with a loved one who is mute with misery and immobilised by depression and despair, what was to be done? Hissing the doctor didn't seem to be the answer and I left the cinema (which wasn't the answer either).

ECT apart, much of the literature to do with mental and neurological illness irritated on a different level and still does. There is a snobbery about mental affliction beginning, I suspect, with Freud; there was little twisting of the cloth cap went on in Freud's consulting room, I'm sure, but it wasn't simply due to social snobbery. Like most writers on the subject, the great man concerned himself with the intellectual and the exotic, so that there was something of the freak show about many of his well-known case histories, with alleviation of suffering nowhere.

Depression, which is much the most common mental

illness, doesn't even qualify as such and mustn't be so labelled, perhaps because it's routine and relatively unshowy; but maybe, too, because it's so widespread not calling depression mental illness helps to sidestep the stigma. A sufferer from it, though, might well regret that his or her condition is so common since a patient mindless with despair is such a regular occurrence as scarcely to be worthy of a proper physician's time.

Nothing excuses us from the obligation to divert our fellow creatures. We must not be boring. And since for the specialist most illnesses soon cease to intrigue, if you have to suffer choose a condition that is rare. Should you want to catch the doctor's eye, the trick is not to see no light at the end of the tunnel; anybody can do that. Rather mistake your wife for a hat and the doctor will never be away from your bedside.

To give them credit, Laing and his followers were not medically snobbish in this way, but what they seldom discussed was the effect an illness like depression had on the rest of the family, in this case my father. The reverse, the effect the family had on the patient, was much discussed and it was one of the central tenets of Laing's writing that mental illness was generally the work and the fault of the family. In the crowded family plot love, or at least relationships, cramped and warped the weak and ailing, with health only to be achieved by explaining how schizophrenia, say, had been a rational response to the constraints that other family members had imposed, this process of explanation invariably leaving the family, if not in the dock, at least a bit shamefaced.

But nothing that I read or saw at that time resembled the situation in our family, the sudden defection of a loved one, her normal personality wiped out with a total loss of nerve. In Laing and in Szasz the love that was on offer in the family was generally seen as rigid and repressive, with affection bartered for good behaviour. This didn't seem to me to have much to do with my father's affection for my mother, which, while not denying her faults, seemed as near selfless as one could get. There was no bargain here that I could see, just distress and loss on both sides. The books talked of the family working through its breakdown and coming to a new understanding, but when both parties were in their mid-sixties it seemed a bit late in the day for that. What Mam and Dad both wanted was the same going-on as they had had before, and if ECT was a short cut to that then they would take it.

We were told that following a few sessions of ECT Mam would be more herself, and progressively so as the treatment went on. In the event improvement was more dramatic. Given her first bout of ECT in the morning, by the afternoon Mam was walking and talking with my father as she hadn't for months. He saw it as a miracle, as I did too, and to hear on the phone the dull resignation gone from his voice and the old habitual cheerfulness back was like a miracle too.

Successive treatments consolidated the improvement and soon she was her old self, confused a little as to how this terrible visitation had come about and over what period, but that and other short-term memory loss could be put down to the treatment. Now for the first time she went back to the cottage for a trial weekend and was straightaway on the phone, bubbling over with its charms and the beauty of the village and particularly how clean everything was.

My mother had fought a war against dirt all her life, as any conscientious housewife had to who lived in one of the industrial towns of the West Riding. To visit Halifax, where she grew up, was, my father always said, like going down into the mouth of hell, the bottom of the valley invisible in a haze of soot and smoke. Leeds was scarcely better, Armley, where we first lived, covered in a fine drizzle of grit from Kirkstall Power Station.

The campaign against this dirt produced its own elaborate weaponry, an armoury of Ewbanks, Hoovers, wringers, possers and mops in daily and wearisome use, items still familiar nowadays because sold in the humbler antique shops, everything in good time collectable. Besides these implements my mother maintained an elaborate hierarchy of cloths, buckets and dusters, to the Byzantine differences of which she alone was privy. Some cloths were dishcloths but not sink cloths; some were for the sink but not for the floor. There were dirty buckets and clean buckets, buckets for indoors, buckets for the flags outside. One mop had universal application, another a unique and terrible purpose and so had to be kept outside hung on the wall. And however rinsed and clean these utensils were they remained polluted by their awful function.

In my television play *Afternoon Off* a husband is visiting his wife in hospital.

MRS BEEVERS: I bet the house is upside down.

MR BEEVERS: Nay, it never is. I did the kitchen floor this morning.

MRS BEEVERS: Which bucket did you use?

MR BEEVERS: The red one.

MRS BEEVERS: That's the outside bucket! I shall have it all to do again. Men, they make work.

Left to himself Dad, like the hapless Mr Beevers, would violate these taboos and use the first thing that came to hand to clean the hearth or wash the floor.

'It's all nowt,' he'd mutter, but when Mam was around he knew it saved time and temper to observe her order of things.

Latterly disposable cloths and kitchen rolls had tended to blur these ancient distinctions but the basic structure remained, perhaps the firmest part of the framework of her world.

When she became depressed the breakdown of this order was one of its first symptoms. She became incapable of cleaning the house herself, and stood by while Dad took over her duties. But however much he washed and tidied, the place was still 'upside down', dust and dirt an unstemmable tide, the house besieged by filth and chaos, its (imagined) squalor a talking point among the neighbours. So now when she came home from the hospital bright and better her first comment was how spotless the place looked. And not merely the house. She was taken up by the freshness of everything. It was as if the whole world and her existence in it had been rinsed clean.

But it did not last.

'I don't know what I've done wrong.'

'You've done nothing wrong.'

'Then why are you shouting at me?'

'I'm shouting at you to try and get it into your head.'

'They'll hear.'

'Who? There's nobody here.'

'Then what's that little car doing?'

'Having a nice time. Leading a normal life. Doing what we used to do.'

In the eight years between the onset of my mother's first depression and my father's death in 1974 there were half a dozen episodes, all of which ended up being what Dad called 'hospital dos' and in half of which she had ECT, other times just antidepressant drugs.

In no case was her recovery quite as dramatic as that first time. Perhaps it was that we were getting used to the sequence, but certainly with each successive visitation it became clear that in her case this wasn't an illness that was ever altogether going to go away, the likelihood of another attack there even in her most cheerful moments.

Still, there were long periods of remission, months, years even, when she was her old cheerful self, though Dad was now always on the lookout for any tell-tale signs and ready to head her off from any experience that might upset her. One night we were watching Jeremy Sandford's TV play *Edna, the Inebriate Woman*. Its elaborate depiction of irrational behaviour had nothing to do with Mam's depressive condition, and the connection never occurred to me, but while she was out of the room Dad quietly switched the television off.

'Oh, are we not watching that?' Mam said, coming back.

'Well,' said Dad, 'it was too far-fetched. You can't believe half the stuff that's on.'

Always there was the shame at the nature of the illness, something Mam was able to overcome or at least ignore when she was well but which became a burden whenever her spirits began to fall, the guilt attendant upon the depression one of the signals that it was returning. Self-consciousness, if not shame, was in such a small community understandable, but the longer my parents lived in the village the more I became aware that my mother was not alone in her condition. Several middle-aged women were similarly afflicted in different degrees, one stumping silently round the village every afternoon, another flitting anxiously into a friendly neighbour's, sometimes in tears, and both suffering from what was still called 'nerves' – a condition that goes largely unnoticed in cities as it cannot do in smaller communities.

'I haven't seen Mrs Bennett about? Is she alright?'

Except that after a while people learned not to ask. And while there were support groups for some identifiable disabilities like MS or muscular dystrophy, there were none for depression. As how could there be? Anyone suffering from it would be incapable of attending.

Insofar as I too kept it quiet when she was poorly, I shared in the shame, though it would have been callous to behave otherwise, as even when she was well Mam was always concerned with 'what folks would say' about every department of our lives. But once she was in hospital there could be no deception as Dad would be seen driving off on the dot of one and arriving back at six, day after day after day.

When Mam was ill the first time I used to wish that they both had had the education they always longed for, feeling, snobbishly perhaps, that mental affliction was more appropriate to, sat more suitably on, someone educated or higher up the social scale. It's a foolish assumption besides being statistically unfounded, which I'm sure I knew at the time though I felt it nevertheless. Education might at least have given them more insight into their predicament and diminished some of the self-consciousness they felt and which I felt too, though only in the village; among my own friends I made no secret of it. Still, if nothing else my mother's depression and the omissions and evasions that attended it made me appreciate more the shame that must have attached to my grandfather's drowning and how it was the episode had gone unspoken of for so long.

My father wore a suit every day of his life. He had two, 'my suit' and 'my other suit', 'my suit' being the one he wore

Wilsill, 1939

every day, 'my other suit' his best. On the rare occasions when he invested in a new suit the suits moved up a place, 'my other suit' becoming 'my suit', the new suit becoming 'my other suit', with the old one just used for painting in or working in the shop. They were three-piece suits, generally navy, and he always wore black shoes and a collar and tie. This makes him seem formal or dressed like an accountant but he didn't give that impression because he never managed to be smart, his waistcoat ('weskit' as he pronounced

Dad, on holiday as a young man

it) generally unbuttoned and showing his braces, his sleeves rolled up, and when he was still butchering the suit would smell of meat, with the trousers and particularly the turn-ups greasy from the floor. He never had an overcoat, just a series of fawn or dark green gaberdine raincoats, and he always wore a dark green trilby hat.

About clothes Dad must always have been conserva-tive.There are photographs of him as a young man, sitting on the sands in a deck-chair in the 1920s, and he is in his three-piece suit, with dicky-bow and fly-collar and even a bowler hat, his only concession to the holiday spirit bare feet. Retirement, which often sanctions some sartorial indulgence, didn't alter this state of affairs, the regime of suit and other suit maintained as before. Or almost.

After he had learned to drive my parents would some-times collect me off the train at Lancaster. Meeting them there one day in 1970, I came across the bridge to see my mother waiting at the barrier with a stranger, someone got up in a grey check sports coat, two-tone cardigan, brown trousers and what I suppose would be called loafers. I was deeply shocked. It was Dad in leisurewear, the only relic of the man he had always been his green trilby hat.

'What do you think of your Dad's new get-up?' Mam enquired as we were driving home. Not much was the truth of it but I didn't let on, and as Dad didn't say much either I took it to have been Mam's idea, confirmed when the experiment turned out to be short-lived; the sports coat and brown trousers soon demoted to the status of garden-ing clothes, and we were back on the regime of 'my suit' and 'my other suit'.

Mam and Dad (in his casuals), Scarborough

Dad's brief excursion into leisurewear wasn't an isolated occurrence but part of a process (Mam would have liked it to have been a programme) called 'branching out'. The aim of 'branching out' was to be more like other people, or like what Mam imagined other people to be, an idea she derived in the first instance from women's magazines and latterly from television. The world of coffee mornings, flower arrangement, fork lunches and having people round for drinks was never one my parents had been part of. Now that Mam was well again and Dad could drive, Mam's modest social ambitions, long dormant, started to revive and she began to entertain the possibility of 'being a bit more like other folks'. The possibility was all it was, though, and much to Dad's relief, all that it remained.

'It's your Dad,' Mam would complain. 'He won't mix. I'd like to, only he won't.'

And there was no sense in explaining to her that these occasions she read about in *Homes and Gardens* were not all that they were cracked up to be, or if it came to the point she'd be nonplussed in company. Other people did it, why couldn't we?

Drink would have helped but both my parents were tee-totallers, though more from taste than conviction. Indeed alcohol had, for Mam at least, a certain romance, partly again to be put down to the cocktail parties she had read about in women's magazines. She had never been to, still less given, a cocktail party, which explains why she could never get the pronunciation of the actual word right, invariably laying the stress on the final syllable, cock*tail*. What a cock*tail* was I am sure she had no idea. Russell Harty used to tell how when he was at Oxford he had invited Vivien Leigh round for drinks and she had asked for pink gin. Only having the plain stuff Russell sent a friend out to the nearest off-licence for a bottle of the pink variety. Mam would not have understood there was a joke here, and had she ever got round to giving a cocktail party she would probably have tried to buy a bottle of cocktails.

The nearest my parents came to alcohol was at Holy Communion and they utterly overestimated its effects. However bad the weather, Dad never drove to church because Mam thought the sacrament might make him incapable on the return journey.

They did, however, gather that sherry was a generally acceptable drink, so once they were settled down in the village they invested in a bottle, as a first move in the 'branching out' campaign.

'Your Dad and me are going to start to mix,' Mam wrote. 'We've got some sherry in and we've got some peanuts too.'

Never having tasted the mysterious beverage, though, they lacked any notion of when it was appropriate and treated it as a round-the-clock facility. Thus the vicar, calling with the Free Will offering envelope, was startled to be offered a sweet sherry at 10 o'clock in the morning. They, of course, stuck to tea; or, when they were trying to fit in, Ribena.

'Well,' said Mam resignedly, 'it doesn't do for us. Our Kathleen used to put it in the trifle and it always rifted up on me.'

On another occasion when they had actually been asked out to drinks and gone in great trepidation Mam rang up in some excitement.

'Your Dad and me have found an alcoholic drink that we really like. It's called bitter lemon.'

Nor was it merely the drink at cocktail parties my mother found mysterious, but the food that was on offer there too – cocktail snacks, bits of cheese and pineapple, sausages-on-sticks, food that nowadays would come under the generic term of nibbles. Now sausages were not unknown in our house: my father had been a butcher after all, we took them in our stride. But a sausage had only to be hoisted onto a stick to become for my mother an emblem of impossible sophistication.

With these notions it's hardly surprising they never made

the social round or lived the kind of model life my mother used to read about in magazines. They put it down, as they did most of their imagined shortcomings, to their not having been educated, education to them a passport to everything they lacked: self-confidence, social ease and above all the ability to be like other people. Every family has a secret and the secret is that it's not like other families. My mother imagined that every family in the kingdom except us sat down together to a cooked breakfast, that when the man of the house had gone off to work and the children to school there was an ordered programme of washing, cleaning, baking and other housewifely tasks, interspersed with coffee mornings and (higher up the social scale) cocktail parties. What my parents never really understood was that most families just rubbed along anyhow.

A kind of yearning underlay both their lives. Before they moved to the village, my father's dream was of a smallholding (always referred to as such). He saw himself keeping hens, a goat, and growing his own potatoes; an idyll of self-sufficiency.

I was in Holland not long ago, where along every railway line and on any spare bit of urban land were hundreds of neat plots, which were not allotments so much as enclosed gardens, each with a hut, a pavilion almost, outside which the largely elderly owners were sunbathing (some of them virtually naked). Dad would never have gone in for that, but I think, though less cheek by jowl, this was just what he meant by a smallholding. It was a dream, of course, of a generation older than his, a vision of the soldiers who survived the First World War, with Surrey, Essex and Kent full of rundown chicken farms, the sad relics of those days.

Dad had no social ambitions, such aspirations as he did have confined to playing his violin better. He read a good deal, though there was never a bookshelf in the living room and all the books in the house were kept in my room, Mam's view being that books not so much furnished a room as untidied it. What books they had of their own were kept in the sideboard, most of them even at this late stage in their lives to do with self-improvement: *How to Improve Your Memory Power, In Tune with the Infinite, Relax Your Way to Health!* After Dad died my brother and I went to collect his belongings from the hospital – his bus pass, a few toffees he'd had in his pocket, and in his wallet a cutting from a newspaper: 'Cure Bronchitis in a Week! Deep Breathing the Only Answer'.

'We're neither of us anything in the mixing line. We were when we were first married, but you lose the knack.'

'Anyway, I don't see what God has to do with mixing. Too much God and it puts the tin hat on it.'

This is an exchange from *Say Something Happened*, a TV play of mine about an oldish couple visited by a young social worker who is worried by their isolation. It never got to the social worker stage with Mam and Dad, but certainly they kept to themselves more and more as they got older and as Mam's depressions became more frequent. Besides, everything was social. They stopped going to church because all too often they got roped in after the service to take part in a discussion group.

'It was a talk on the Third World,' Dad wrote to me. 'Well, your Mam and me don't even know where the Third World is. Next week it's Buddhism. We're going to give it a miss.'

Small talk, Buddhism, sausages-on-sticks, like the second name he did not want Gordon to have, they were for other people, not for them.

With Mam, though, the dream of sociability persisted. When, after Dad died, she went to live with my brother, I was clearing out the kitchen cupboard, and there behind an old bottle of Goodall's Vanilla Essence and a half-empty packet of Be-Ro Self-Raising Flour I came across a sad little tube of cocktail sticks.

Put simply and as they themselves would have put it, both my parents were shy, a shortcoming they thought of as an affliction while at the same time enshrining it as a virtue. Better to be shy, however awkward it made you feel, than be too full of yourself and always shoving yourself forward.

It may have been shyness that drew my parents together in the first place; my mother was shy as her sisters were not and my father was the least outgoing of his brothers. The early morning wedding at St Bartholomew's, Armley, was a ceremony for a couple shy of ceremony, so it's not surprising if in the years that followed a premium was put on shy and it became our badge.

Half of Dad's morality came out of his shyness, reinforcing as it did the modesty of his expectations while resigning him to the superior enterprise and good fortune of others.

'Your Dad won't push himself forward,' Mam would say, 'that's his trouble.' That it was her trouble too was not the point; she was a woman, after all. Thus he seldom got angry and, too shy to tell anybody off, just 'felt sickened'. Regularly cheated or done down in business, he never became hardened to it or came by a philosophy to cope, other than doing imitations of the people he disliked, longing to give them 'Joe Fitton's remedy'* or just being funny generally. But he chafed against a temperament that made him much liked by everyone except himself, and it's not surprising that, suppressing his real feelings, he was a martyr to stomach trouble, a complaint, along with the shyness, he has bequeathed to me.

Shyness (which will keep cropping up in this book) is a soft word, foggy and woollen, and it throws its blanket over all sorts of behaviour. It covers a middle-aged son or neurasthenic daughter living at home with an elderly mother, through to some socially crippled and potentially

---

* During the war Dad was a warden in the ARP, his companion on patrol a neighbour, Joe Fitton. Somebody aroused Joe's ire (a persistent failure to draw their blackout curtains, perhaps), and one night, having had to ring the bell and remonstrate yet again, Joe burst out, 'I'd like to give them a right kick up the arse.' This wasn't like Joe at all and turned into a family joke – and a useful one too, as Dad never swore, so to give somebody a kick up the arse became euphemistically known as 'Joe Fitton's remedy'. With Dad it even became a verb: 'I'd like to Joe Fitton him.'

dangerous creature incapable of human response; shy a spectrum that stretches from the wallflower to the psychopath. 'A bit of a loner' is how the tabloids put it after some shrinking wreck has ventured to approach or make off with a child or exposed himself in a park, 'shy' thought altogether too kindly a description. Because 'soft' comes near it, and 'timid', too, but without the compassion or understanding implicit in shy. That he or she is shy is an excuse or an extenuation that is made by others (mothers in particular) but seldom by the persons concerned. Because if you are shy then you're generally too shy to say so, 'I'm shy' a pretty bold thing to come out with.

Sheltering under shy, it was a long time before I understood that the self-effacing and the self-promoting, shy and its opposite, share a basic assumption, shy and forward the same. Everybody is looking at me, thinks the shy person (and I wish they weren't). Everybody is looking at me, thinks the self-confident (and quite right too). I learned this lesson in time to be able to point it out, probably rather sententiously, to my parents, but it was too late for them, and the other lesson I had learned, that to be shy was to be a bit of a bore, they knew already, to their cost. I assured them, falsely, that everybody felt much as they did but that social ease was something that could and should be faked.

'Well, you can do that,' Dad would say, 'you've been educated,' adding how often he felt he had nothing to contribute. 'I'm boring, I think. I can't understand why anybody likes us. I wonder sometimes whether they do, really.'

I found this heartbreaking because it wasn't said with an eye to being told the opposite. It was genuinely how they thought of themselves.

Left out of this account are all their jokes and fun, the pleasure they got out of life and their sheer silliness. After retirement they both put on weight, and coming in one day I found them sitting side by side on the sofa. 'Here we are,' said Dad, 'Fat Pig One and Fat Pig Two.'

Dad had always been shy about sex, never talking about it directly and disapproving of any reference to it by us as children or even of Mam's occasional 'cheeky' remark. I was used to this and respected it, except that I was not immune to some of the modish stuff talked about mental illness in the seventies and at some point on one of the long drives to and from the hospital I heard myself asking my father if he touched my mother enough. He was too embarrassed to reply, 'Nay, Alan' all that he'd commit himself to, the implication being what business was it of mine. And he was quite right. Who was I to ask what amount of touching went on, who at that time had touched and was touching virtually no one at all? It might have been better, more acceptable as a question, had I said hugging rather than touching, but hugging as a manifestation of (often unfeeling) affection had not yet achieved the currency it did in the eighties and nineties when it often served to demonstrate that other loveless construct, caring. The thought of myself putting the question at all makes me wince in retrospect, but how should I ask about hugging when I knew, as he did, that none of our family were great huggers, though no less affectionate for that.

Dad would have been shy to have been seen embracing Mam, but when I put to him the unnecessary question about touching he could, unthinkably, have retorted that, though it was nothing to do with me, at seventy he still was actually touching Mam when and where it mattered. This emerged a year or two later, in 1974, when he was lying in Intensive Care in the same Airedale Hospital recovering, as we were assured, from a heart attack. Mam had only just been discharged from the same hospital and was at home coming round after yet another bout of depression. Dazed by her own illness and stunned by his, she lay in bed talking about Dad, sometimes, as was not uncommon when she was poorly, taking me for him. Out of the blue she suddenly said,

'He does very well, you know, your Dad.'

'Yes,' I said, taking this for a general statement.

'No. I mean for a fellow of seventy-one.'

Again I did not twig.

'Why?'

'Well, you know when we were in Leeds he had to have that little operation to do with his water. Well, most fellers can't carry on much after that. But it didn't make any difference to your Dad. He does very well.'

Had I known it, the pity was all in the tense, since his doing, however well, was now almost done, and he died a few days later.

'It was only on Tuesday he drove us over to Morecambe,' said Mam. 'It was miserable all day, only it fined up at tea time so we thought we'd have a run-out. Will it be all the driving to the hospital that's done it?'

I said I didn't think so, though I did.

'We went up to the West End by the golf course. I wanted a bit of a walk on the sands but we'd only been going a minute when he said, "Nay, Mam, you'll have to stop. I can't go no further." It must have been coming on then.'

I knew exactly the place where they would have been walking. It was up towards Bare, the suburb of Morecambe always thought 'a bit more select'. We had walked on the same sands often, particularly during the war, when all our seaside holidays seemed to be taken at Morecambe. For Dad they were scarcely a holiday at all, as with no one to stand in for him at the Co-op he never managed more than a couple of days, a break so short it was always overshadowed by the grief-stricken leave-taking with which it invariably concluded. The sadness of these partings ought to have been comic, though it never seemed so. Having seen him off on the train the three of us would walk on the empty evening sands as the sun set across the bay, and Mam wept and wept. For what? They were only to be separated four or five days at the most, and Dad wasn't going back to the front but to dreary old Leeds, which seldom even ran to an air raid. It was love, I suppose, and the loneliness of a week with her two uncomforting boys.

So that these sands, where once she had wept so bitterly and grieved so needlessly, should now be the setting for their last walk together seems, if not fitting, then at least symmetrical, the disproportionate grief then finding its appropriate object forty years later, the equation complete.

Afterwards I came to think I might have been in some degree responsible, and that Dad's death was my doing if not my fault. Already written in 1974, though not filmed, was my second TV play, *Sunset Across the Bay,* where I had included a scene in which a retired couple say farewell to their son, who is going off to Australia. I set the goodbye on that same stretch of Morecambe sand before, in a later scene, killing off the father with a stroke in a seafront lavatory. The couple in the play have retired to Morecambe from Leeds and were not unlike my parents, except that whereas in the play their lives are lonely and unhappy and their expectations from retirement unfulfilled, Mam and Dad's retirement, even with Mam's depression, was one of the happiest times of their lives. We made the film that autumn, by which time Dad was three months dead, his first heart attack one

Saturday morning in August 1974, the second a week later killing him.

Anyone who writes will be familiar with the element of involuntary prediction that informs the imagination; one writes about something, and if it does not exactly happen a version of it does. Sometimes, when one is writing about oneself, for instance, there is an objective explanation; it was only after writing a play that dealt, albeit farcically, with sexual inhibition that my own sex life picked up, the play a form of crude psychotherapy, 'getting it out of your system' (or 'off your chest') another way of putting it.

That by writing a play about the death of a father I brought on the death of my own is perhaps fanciful, though the thought certainly occurred. But there were other, less notional ways, too, in which I may have contributed to his dying.

The heart attack had not been without warning, but all attention, Dad's included, had been so concentrated on Mam's situation and her recurring depressions that his own failing health went unconsidered, at any rate by me, and he, typically, said nothing on the phone. Or did he? Maybe I didn't want to hear.

I had been taking the journey north less often than previously because I was acting in *Habeas Corpus* in the West End, the only way to get home to drive up on the Sunday and back on the Monday, so if I was neglecting my duties there was some excuse. Still, it was an excuse, and the truth was I was reluctant to be away from London even for a night because I was having a nice time, and what was more, knew it. I was 'living' as one of the characters in another play describes it, the play being *Intensive Care*, in which a father has a heart attack and his son sits at his hospital bedside in order to be with him when he dies, but at the crucial moment is not with his father but in bed with a nurse. I am not I and he is not he, but I could see where that play, written six years later, came from.

I had always been a late starter and aged forty, and in the nick of time as it seemed to me then, I had caught up with that sexual revolution which, so Philip Larkin (who was not a reliable witness) claimed, had begun a decade earlier. While sexual intercourse did not quite begin in 1974 it was certainly the year when sex was available pretty much for the asking . . . or maybe I had just learned the right way to ask. Whatever the reason, I suddenly seemed to be leading the kind of life I was told everybody else had been leading for years. I had at last, as they say, got it together. It was at this point my father died and I was summarily banished from London, where such things were possible, to live with my mother in Yorkshire, where they were not.

It was not quite as sudden as that, as a week intervened between his first attack and the second. I went up straightaway to find him in Intensive Care, tired but said to be on the mend. *Habeas Corpus* had only half a dozen performances left so I was going back to London to finish the run, and also to resume my suddenly eventful existence, at least for as long as I was allowed to. On my way I called at the hospital to say goodbye and to tell him that I'd see him in a week's time. He was propped up in bed, his pyjama jacket open, the electrodes that monitored his heart attached to his chest. I don't think he ever sunbathed in his life or even wore an open-necked shirt and the line of his collar was sharp, his worn red face and neck like a helmet above the creamy whiteness of his chest.

We never kissed much in our family; I kissed my mother often but I don't ever recall kissing my father since I was a boy. Even when we were children Dad would make a joke of kissing, pulling a face and sticking his cheek out to indicate the exact spot on which this distasteful task had to be carried out. Seeing him less often than I did, my brother would shake hands, but I can't recall ever doing that either. Which is not to say that we were remote from each other, and indeed I felt much closer to him grown up than I ever did as a child when, smart and a show-off, I often felt myself an embarrassment and not the child he would have wanted.

So I sat for a while at his bedside and then stood up to say goodbye. And uniquely in my adulthood, kissed him on the cheek. Seeing the kiss coming he shifted slightly, and I saw a look of distant alarm in his eyes, on account not just of the kiss but of what it portended. I was kissing him, he clearly thought, because I did not expect to see him again. He knew it for what it was and so did I, because somebody had once done the same to me.[*] It was the kiss of death.

If I could wipe away that kiss and the memory of it I would do, though trusting in the doctor's prognosis I had no thought that Dad was likely to die. I fear what made me kiss him was again the fashionable nonsense about families being healthier for touching and showing affection, the

* See 'A Common Assault', in *The Uncommon Reader*, p. 557

same modish stuff that had made me ask him if he touched my mother. And it was something similar that made me ask after his death if I might see his body. It was death as the last taboo, death as much a part of life as birth, all the up-to-the-minute Sunday papers stuff. Less forgivably there was some notion that being a writer demanded an unflinching eye, to look on death part of the job. Besides, I was forty and the death of the father was one of the great formative experiences; I had a duty to make the most of it.

He had died on the Saturday morning when I was already on the train north, so when I saw his body on the Monday at Airedale Hospital he had been dead two days. The mortuary was somewhere at the back of the hospital; not a facility I suppose they wanted to make a show of, it was near the boiler room and the back doors of the kitchens. I was put into a curtained room (called the viewing room) where Dad lay under a terrible purple pall. There were two attendants, one of whom pulled back the shroud. It was a shocking sight. His face had shrunk and his teeth no longer fitted so that his mouth was set in a snarl, a look about as uncharacteristic of him as I could ever have imagined. It was the first time in his life (except that it wasn't in his life) that he can have looked fierce. I noticed that the attendants were looking at me, more interested in my reactions than in the corpse which to them must have been commonplace. Noting that at seventy-one he still had scarcely a grey hair, I nodded and they wheeled him out.

Back in London for a couple of days I mentioned my father's death to Miss Shepherd, the tramp on the street who, a few months before, had moved her van into my garden. She did not trouble to express any sympathy, never altogether crediting the misfortune of anyone but herself. Nor in this case.

'Yes. I knew he must have died. I saw him a few days ago. He was hovering over the convent at the top of the street. I think it was to warn you against the dangers of Communism.'

This vision was only slightly more implausible than its purported purpose. I could think of many reasons why my father might have been hovering around at the top of the street ('Try and be more patient with your Mam' for instance) but the Red Menace would have come very low down on the list.

My father's was not the only corpse I was to see that summer of 1974. Within a month I came across another body and in circumstances where even the terrible purple pall that covered my father would not have been unwelcome. But to tell that tale means going back to the forties and catching up on my aunties.

There were three aunties on my mother's side of the family, the Peels, which was the side of the family we saw most of. There were three aunties on my father's side too, the wives of his three Bennett brothers, but we saw much less of them. This was because, the Gimmer's fireside hardly being a welcoming one, no sooner had Dad started courting Mam than he was drawn into the far friendlier family of his fiancée. And this was the pattern for the rest of their lives, with us seeing far more of the Peels than we ever did of the Bennetts.

No one could have been less like the conventional mother-in-law than Grandma Peel and she was, for my father, very much the mother he had never had. Tall, dignified and straightforward, she was in every sense a big woman who had come through the tragedies of her life unembittered and with her sense of humour intact; she had seen two

Grandma Peel

bankruptcies, her family reduced from relative affluence to abject poverty, the death of her only son in the trenches, and the never-spoken-of suicide of her husband which left her with three daughters to bring up on very little, and yet she remained a funny, self-sufficient, lively woman. Dad would never hear a word against her, so that when as a child I heard comedians making stock mother-in-law jokes I was mystified: who were these carping, cantankerous, fault-finding creatures, the bane of their sons-in-law's lives? I'd never come across one.

My mother's sisters were Kathleen and Lemira, both resident at Gilpin Place: Kathleen the oldest, Lemira the youngest, my mother, Lilian, the one in the middle. ('That was the trouble,' she used to say of her childhood, 'I got it from both sides.') Writing about them, I feel a twinge of snobbish regret that they were invariably called 'Aunty' and never 'Aunt'. Aunts, after all, are women to be taken seriously; they are, at the very least, middle class and come equipped with a long literary pedigree; aunties, on the other hand, have no lineage or standing at all. However you look at it, an aunty is an aunt cosified; even a literary dreadnought like Lady Bracknell would lose half her firepower were she Aunty Augusta. So the seriousness of a narrative like this in which my mother's sisters figure pretty continuously seems, as I say snobbishly, cheapened by calling them aunties. Best to forget the relationship altogether then; except that, brought up never to call grown-ups by anything so naked as their name, I could no more write plain Kathleen and Myra than I could have ever called them that to their faces. Moreover, shorn of their status such untitled creatures would not resemble the women I remember. No. Aunties it has to be.

We did have one aunt, though, Aunt Eveline, and she was preserved from diminishment into Aunty by her age – she was Grandma Peel's sister-in-law – by her demeanour, which was imposing, and by her build, which was stout. The word was hers, and it was dinned into my brother and me as children not only that we should never refer to Aunt Eveline in her presence as fat, which we would in any case have been unlikely to do, but – a much taller order – never even refer to anyone else in her presence as fat. This was particularly unfair because, had Aunt Eveline not thought of herself as fat, had fatness not been put on the agenda as it were, I'm sure it would never have occurred to us. She was just Aunt Eveline, her size (which was not exceptional) something we took for granted.

In retrospect I see that Aunt Eveline's problem was her large, undifferentiated bust, a bust that echoed the lid of the piano on which she was such an accomplished performer. It was this bust that until the brink of adolescence confused me about the female anatomy. Aunt Eveline's breasts were so large as to make the cleavage between them resemble a deep, damp-looking canyon, a shaft going down into the recesses of the body like the entrance to Gaping Ghyll. I knew vaguely about the shaft at the other end of the body, but there can be few boys who thought as I did, at the age of eleven, that the female anatomy includes a kind of pectoral vagina. And that the naked woman at the front of *Everybody's Home Doctor*, standing with her palms towards you 'showing all she'd got', displayed no trace of such an orifice did not entirely dislodge the idea from my mind. Aunt Eveline was wont to screen the entrance to this mysterious shaft with an embroidered frontal not unlike the linen antimacassars on the back of the three-piece suite in the sitting room, between the backs of the easy chairs and Aunt Eveline's broad bust there not being much to choose.

Aunt Eveline was 'a lovely pianist' and had beautiful handwriting, her name and address in Pellon Lane, Halifax, written on the covers of all the music in the piano stool. She had had a brief career playing the piano in the silent cinema, then, when the talkies came in, had turned corsetière, a profession often embraced by ample ladies who could simultaneously model the product they were marketing. She still had a connection with corsets in the early forties but by this time she had turned housekeeper, looking after a Mr Wilson, a rich Bradford widower and former chairman of the Bradford Dyers' Association. Widower isn't a designation men would readily apply to themselves these days, and housekeeping as a profession seems to have gone out too. In those days, though, housekeeping covered a multitude of sins, but not, I think, in Aunt Eveline's case. Mr Wilson was well off and already had one fancy woman, whose doings and dresses would be scathingly described over high tea at Gilpin Place, together with the slights Aunt Eveline had suffered at this shameless creature's hands and what Aunt Eveline ('I was scrupulously polite') had rejoindered. Even aged ten I knew Aunt Eveline's hostility to this fancy woman owed less to outraged respectability than to Aunt Eveline's desire to be in her shoes, though it was hard to see why as on the only occasion we were led into her employer's presence ('Mr Wilson, may I introduce my great-nephews') I thought I had never seen anyone who looked more like a toad . . . or, as it might have occurred to me later, a character out of Priestley or John Braine. Oddly, his photo has ended up in the family archives, though Aunt Eveline's main bequest to us when she died in 1956 was her piano and the sheet music that came with it.

While Grandma is alive family Sunday evenings at Gilpin Place follow a settled routine, with the four of us coming over to Wortley from Headingley (Number 1 tram to City Square, Number 12 to Fourteenth Avenue), where we would have high tea and then go to church at St Mary's. Dad would see his brother George, who sang in the choir, and afterwards they would adjourn to the sitting room at Gilpin Place.

There were always flowers in the sitting room, bought at Sleights, the greengrocer's at the corner of Green Lane and Tong Road; huge chrysanthemums (sixpence a bloom), carnations (threepence a spray) arranged in glass celery vases, and anemones in one of Grandma's many lustre jugs.

The chrysanthemums often had as backing another flower, which I never knew had a name and didn't much care for because it smelled to me of decay. I went to France first at the age of twenty and suddenly, hitchhiking near Cahors, I caught a whiff of it from a nearby field and realised it must be mimosa, for some a scent that means the Côte d'Azur but for me redolent of the front room of a sooty Leeds back-to-back.

The sitting room would also smell of smoke as the fire would have been lit by transferring a load of hot coals from the kitchen, a dramatic and dangerous proceeding, the children told to keep back as Grandma bore through the smoking shovel with one of the aunties following in her wake to retrieve any stray coals.

'Now then, Walter,' Aunt Eveline would say. 'What shall we give them?' though the truth was they were performing more for their own pleasure than for ours, particularly as the performance curtailed conversation. While Aunt Eveline was playing talking was out, a severe deprivation for Aunty Kathleen and Aunty Myra, who could only keep up an appearance of musical appreciation for so long before retreating to the kitchen to get on with their gabbing.

There was no self-consciousness about these musical evenings, and no sense that they were the last throes of a tradition that radio had dented but which within ten years television would put paid to altogether. Dad liked playing, Uncle George loved singing and Aunt Eveline, who seldom got a chance to play in company, came over from Bradford specially for the treat. As a child, of course, I found it all very boring, though it endowed me with a comprehensive

Among the marigolds in Grandma's garden, Gilpin Place, 1947

knowledge of the works of Ivor Novello, Vivian Ellis and Gilbert and Sullivan, not to mention Edwardian favourites like Albert Ketèlbey. I have only to hear 'I can give you the moon, I can give you the stars' or 'Fly home little heart' and I am back in the sitting room in 1949, crammed into the corner of the sofa, with Dad and his fiddle on one side of the piano, Uncle George and his beaming brick-red face on the other and in between Aunt Eveline's unmentionable bottom overflowing from the piano stool. Uncle George had his special party pieces, generally kicking off with 'Bless This House', which always found favour and which might sometimes provoke a few tears. Then there would be 'And did you not see my lady, go down the garden singing?' with no notion in any of our minds that this was by Handel and therefore a cut above 'In a Monastery Garden', say. There would be selections from Edward German, with 'Rose of England' another solo spot for Uncle George, and then Aunt Eveline would finish off with a medley from *HMS Pinafore* and perhaps a hymn or two. She would rise, flushed, from the piano stool and we'd all have a cup of tea and a bit of cake before she took herself off to Bradford and another week's housekeeping.

{ 108 }

Aunty Kathleen in manageress mode

The aunties resident at Gilpin Place, Aunty Kathleen and Aunty Myra, were both what they were pleased to call career girls, which is to say shop assistants – Kathleen in Manfield's shoe shop on Commercial Street, Myra at White's Ladies' Mantles just across the road in Briggate. Kathleen was always said to be, said herself to be, the manageress of Manfield's, though I suspect this wasn't an official title but simply meant that she was the longest-serving of the women assistants. Longest-suffering too, as in those days buying shoes involved more what nowadays would be called inter-action, the stock not laid out on racks for all to see and try on but secreted in banks of floor-to-ceiling boxes which were often accessible only on ladders, the assistants up and down them as nimble as sailors on the rigging. Customers, whatever their class, were deferentially treated ('Madam takes a broad fitting? Certainly') and off they would go up the ladder again.

It's a sign of my age that shoe shops seem nowadays to be staffed by sluts, indifferent, unhelpful and with none of that matronly dignity with which the selling of shoes and the buying of clothes were in those days conducted. It is a small loss, though buying shoes in a provincial town in Italy a few years ago I noted that none of the assistants was under forty, and all happy and helpful, and it made me remember Manfield's and realise such ladies are a loss, and that in some of what the papers call 'sections of the economy' the right age for a particular job (not that retailers will ever acknowledge it) is often middle age.

The personnel and politics of Manfield's are well known

to us as after work Aunty Kathleen will often come up to Halliday Place and give us her regular bulletin on what has been happening at the shop, recounting the events of her day in Proustian detail. She has a characteristic way of talking, which has been developed as an almost Darwinian response to people's reluctance to listen to the lengthy and often formless narratives she likes to embark on. These are therefore punctuated by phrases like 'If you see what I mean, Lilian', 'If you follow me, Walter' or 'As it subsequently transpired', little verbal tags and tugs just to make sure the person she is talking to is still trotting at the heels of the interminable saga of what she said to the customer and what the customer said to her and what her friend, Miss Moore, said about it all afterwards. And when, after an evening dominated by these narratives, the door finally closes on her Dad blurts out, 'I wouldn't care, but you're no further on when she's done.'

'Yes, but Dad,' Mam chips in, 'she's very good-hearted.' Which indeed she was, but she was a marathon talker.

Unmarried though they are, Kathleen and Myra are hardly maiden aunts, literally or figuratively, and strait-laced is the last thing they want to seem. Less pretty than

'This fellow's taking our picture. Don't look.'

Mam, the aunties are in my brother's and my eyes much more glamorous, seeing themselves as dashing, adventuresome creatures, good sports and always on for what they see as a lark. They wear scent and camiknickers and have the occasional drink, which we are allowed to taste or are given a shandy instead. They even smoke if the occasion requires it and revel in the small sophistications of the single life. They see themselves as women of the world with Bette Davis as their model, over-polite sarcasm and a talent for putting someone in their place skills of which they are both proud. They are big fans of the Duke of Windsor, Aunty Myra in particular giving the impression that, if things hadn't worked out well with Mrs Simpson, HRH could have done worse than marry her.

In those days aunties, particularly of the unmarried sort (and perhaps only if they are unmarried), serve in the family set-up as ladies of misrule. Untrammelled by domestic responsibilities with no husband whose line they have to toe, they are (or fancy themselves) freer spirits than their wifely sisters to whom, in turn, they are slightly suspect, blamed for 'putting ideas into the children's heads' or 'getting them all excited'. These sisters of subversion give their nephews and nieces forbidden foods, dismissing as 'fuss' well-founded parental prohibitions: 'Our Alan can't do with oatcakes, he comes out in heat spots' or 'They don't have fish and chips at night, it keeps them awake'.

In these dismal back streets the aunties' role is as exponents of a hard-won glamour that means wearing more lipstick than Mam ever wears, higher heels, having access to nylons, and if not, painting them on. They go to the second house at the pictures, which we never do, and the occasional dance at the Clock. They may even do things undreamed of with members of the armed forces and get airmail letters from distant parts to prove it. With their swept-up hair and peep-toe sling-backs, regularly consulting their powder compacts, repairing their lipstick and tapping out cigarettes, they are everything that mothers are not, agents of an approximate sophistication and a sooty, provincial chic that makes a sister like my mother who has managed 'to get herself a man' seem conventional and dull.

Renegades who do not subscribe to the grown-ups' pact that censors gossip in front of children, they let fall criticism of other grown-ups that Mam and Dad are careful to avoid when we're around. They even imply that parents themselves are not above criticism, and can be judged as other people are.

'Your mother was always one to carry on', 'They've always been worriers, your Mam and Dad' – judgements one didn't want to hear or wasn't ready to hear, parents still set apart and not subject to the shortcomings and disablements that diminished other people. Parents were the standard still.

Subversion could come in other forms, with an aunty picking up on a nephew or niece's aspirations that are overlooked at home, taking them to the theatre, say, or to 'A' pictures and even pictures in French. Though an aunty's own reading may not stretch much beyond *Rebecca* or the novels of Phyllis Bentley (read with a quarter of Quality Street to hand), it's enough to license her to preach the charms of the literary life and the glamour of those that lead it and to stamp her as a different sort of woman. Russell Harty had just such an aunty, Aunty Alice, who played a large part in his education. Widowed and with no children, she had friends in the choral society and took him to concerts and, if only implicitly, advertised the charms of a different way of life than he got at home, where both his parents worked on the market and never let him forget it.

My own aunties were never quite like this. True, Aunty Myra used to see herself as sensitive and poetry-loving, but since my parents were fond of reading and always liked music Aunty Myra used slyly to hint that these preoccupations, which she led you to believe came naturally to her but had been 'thwarted', were in my mother's case 'put on', casting Mam and Dad as parents who did not appreciate the potential of their own children. This must have been provoking to say the least but, as with the tedium attendant on Aunty Kathleen's footwear narratives, my parents kept their thoughts to themselves, only sharing them with us when we were old enough to sympathise and make the aunties' aspirations a family joke.

Both Aunty Kathleen and Aunty Myra have occasional boyfriends though none seem ever to be brought home, the only indication that something may be going on the frequency with which their names come up in conversation. There are stand-bys like Bill Walsh, a body-building young man who lives in the shadow of Armley Gaol and whose picture in a posing-pouch another that resides incongruously among the family photographs. He had been taken prisoner during the war and had been in a camp in Germany and, so

Aunty Myra says, been put before a firing squad only for his name to be called out and him reprieved at the last moment.

'Well,' said Dad, 'the Germans must have known your aunties were running short of stuff to talk about.'

This, though, was a comment made long afterwards, and while we are children Dad keeps his misgivings to himself . . . or to Mam and himself. What galls him, and I suppose her, is that compared with their dashing, venturesome selves the aunties cast Mam as the sister who is timid and conventional. To some extent she is, though one of the conventions (and the one that galls them) is of course marriage, which neither of them has yet attained. My mother sees their contact with us, and particularly with my brother, who, less bookish and more boyish than me, is more in their line, as a continuation of the sisters' efforts to squash her, which had disfigured her childhood (and from which marriage had delivered her). But if my parents feel this they say nothing to my brother and me, the convention that adults and particularly adult relatives are not criticised in front of the children stronger than any resentment they are feeling. Besides, it is always unwise to let anything out in my presence as, show-off that I am, I am always ready to blab it out if I think it will bring me the limelight, however briefly. My aunties are less discreet than my parents, and I'm sure many an unconsidered remark about Mam when she was a girl or even Mam now is smugly reported back by me. During the war I often think how lucky I am to have been born in England and not to be living in an occupied country or even Germany itself. In fact it is my parents who are the lucky ones as I am the kind of child who, always attention-seeking, would quite happily betray them to the Gestapo if it meant getting centre stage.

For Aunty Myra the war comes as a godsend, and Mr Chamberlain has scarcely finished his broadcast when she is off like a pigeon from a coop. Enlisting in the WAAF, she is posted round the country to various enlistment and maintenance units so that we soon become familiar with the names of hitherto unheard-of places like Innsworth and Hednesford, Formby and Kidbrooke, until in 1943 she is posted to India, thus confirming her role as the adventurous one in the family.

One of the aunties' favourite films was *Now, Voyager* (1942). Mam liked it too but would have liked it more if

Aunty Myra in the WAAF

Charles Boyer had been in it rather than Paul Henreid. I must have seen it at the time, probably at the Picturedrome on Wortley Road, though without caring for it much or even remembering it except as a film Aunty Kathleen and Aunty Myra went on about. But seeing it again recently I began to understand, as perhaps even they didn't, some of the reasons why it appealed to them, and I wrote about it in my diary.

Christmas Eve, 1996. Catch *Now, Voyager* on afternoon TV, watch part and record the rest. Bette Davis was always a favourite of Aunty Kathleen and Aunty Myra and this tale of a dowdy Boston spinster, Charlotte Vale, who finds herself on the high seas and falls into the arms of Paul Henreid seemed to them a promise of what life might hold in store. Perhaps my mother thought so too, though she was never as big a fan of Bette Davis as her sisters, and since she was married and had children she expected less of life.

For Aunty Myra the promise could be said to have come true, as it did for thousands of women who enlisted in the early forties. The first shot of Charlotte Vale is of her sensible-shoed feet and thick, stockinged legs coming hesitantly down the staircase of her tyrannical mother's grand house in Boston. It's echoed a little later in the film when we see another pair of legs, slim and silk-stockinged, stepping elegantly down a gangplank as the camera pans up to reveal a transformed Charlotte gazing from under a huge and glamorous hat, with what seems like poise but is actually shyness, at her fellow passengers on a cruise liner. Aunty Myra's mother, Grandma Peel, was anything but tyrannical and Aunty Myra neither hesitant nor shy, but a year or so after she would have seen *Now Voyager* she made the same transition herself and exchanged the dark shiny-wallpapered stairs at Gilpin Place for the gangway of a cruise liner, stepping down her own gangplank to set foot on tropical shores when she disembarked at Bombay – though less elegantly than Bette Davis, and probably lugging her own kitbag as an LAC in the WAAF.

Christmas Day, 1996. Wake early as I always do these days, and in the absence of a newspaper watch the rest of *Now Voyager,* finding more resonances this time than I had remembered. The shipboard romance with Paul Henreid over, Charlotte Vale, the ex-Aunt Charlotte, returns to Boston and revisits the sanatorium where her benevolent psychiatrist, Dr Jaquith, played by Claude Rains, had helped her to find herself. Seeing a miserable-looking child there she befriends her, the child, of course, turning out to be Tina, the daughter of Durrance, her shipboard lover. Seeing the child as her own once-unloved self, Charlotte takes over her treatment, virtually adopting her, becoming her aunt, until in the final scene the ex-lovers meet at a party at Charlotte's grand Boston home and dedicate their (for the time being) separate futures to the welfare of the now-blossoming child, the film ending with the line:

'And will you be happy, Charlotte?'

'Oh, Jerry. Don't let's ask for the moon. We have the stars.'

This relationship between Charlotte Vale, the ex-aunt and the child, Tina, mirrors the way Aunty Kathleen and Aunty Myra saw themselves, Miss Vale as Miss Peel, coming on as they both did as bolder and more fun-loving and at the same time more sensitive than their married sister, casting Mam and Dad as parents who did not appreciate their own children. This takes us back to *Now Voyager* and the mysterious wife of Jerry Durrance who is spoken of but, like Daphne du Maurier's Rebecca, remains an off-screen presence though she, presumably, would have her own story to tell, and one in which Charlotte Vale might be less kindly regarded.

Aunty Kathleen probably longs to kick over the traces like her sister, but she is nearly forty when the war starts and unmarried, and as the breadwinner has to stay at home to look after Grandma. Her war service takes her no further than Armley Baths and her St John Ambulance Brigade classes; still, it's a uniform and that's what matters. Mam doesn't even get that far but then she has children and neither she nor Dad has any military ambitions, Dad only too relieved that his job as a butcher is a reserved occupation, thus making him immune from the call-up.

For a few years he is an air-raid warden, but raids on Leeds being relatively uncommon his duties are light: a short walk round the Hallidays to check the blackout and the rest of the evening spent playing billiards up at the wardens' post. Mam half-heartedly knits some lurid squares to be made into blankets and we occasionally trail over to the Ministry of Pensions hospital in Chapel Allerton to visit slightly mystified wounded soldiers, but otherwise hostilities scarcely impinge. War, peace, it makes no difference, our family never quite joining in, let alone joining up, and the camaraderie passes us by as camaraderie generally did.

In one sense Aunty Kathleen's membership of the Ambulance Brigade proves a disappointment to me. She is issued with a first-aid handbook which she seldom seems to consult and which with its black and silver lettering hangs about the sideboard at Gilpin Place for the rest of the war. Unlike other medical texts it proves to have little information about the relations between the sexes, not even the stylised nude drawing (the man with a loincloth) that formed the frontispiece of *Everybody's Home Doctor*. Of course on that point, according to Aunty Kathleen's as-always over-detailed account, no instruction was needed. The sessions are held in Armley Baths, the big swimming bath boarded over for the duration and so available for functions. There is no thought in my mind that the bath will have been drained first and I imagine the water gleaming evilly in the darkness under the floor, as between the boards the sea did when we walked along Morecambe Pier to hear the concert party. Manfield's or Armley Baths, Dad has no time for either, but there is no escape as, with her usual 'If you follow me, Lilian' and 'As it went on to transpire', Kathleen tells the tale of these first-aid sessions, now and again shrieking with laughter, the wounded who were not wounded laid out on the beds all the better it seemed to be saucy.

'With all due respect,' says Mr Turnbull in *A Chip in the Sugar*, 'you're not supposed to move a person until it's been ascertained no bones are broken. I was in the St John Ambulance Brigade.'

'Yes,' said mother, 'and who did you learn your bandaging on?' And they both cracked out laughing.

That was what the war was like, in Armley anyway, peals of dirty laughter, middle-aged men in navy-blue battledress making jokes you didn't understand with women who weren't their wives, and nobody seeming to mind. For the duration: 1939, open brackets; 1945, close brackets.

There is not much new furniture to be bought just after the war, all of it bearing the obligatory Utility stamp of two stylised Cs; what they stand for I never know or even wonder. Though some Utility furniture is well designed (and now probably ranks as collectable), Aunty Kathleen picks out an armchair that has no pretensions to style or beauty; it is squat and square with cushioned seat and back, and arms broad enough to conceal cupboards, one of which is intended to serve as a cocktail cabinet and the other as a receptacle for newspapers and magazines. There is even a drawer to hold a cigarette box.

Excitedly anticipating Aunty Myra's return from India in 1946, Kathleen demonstrates how Myra will be installed on this monstrous throne, which will slowly, to her demobbed surprise, yield up its secrets – the drawer filled with Craven A, the cupboard containing a bottle of milk stout (Grandma's not running to cocktails), and the magazine compartment with its copy of *Lilliput*. Thus, ceremonially enthroned in front of the kitchen fire, LAC/2 Peel will know that she has come home.

'What a common thing!' Mam said as soon as we are safely out of the house, a cocktail cabinet, even if it only housed milk stout, always a focus for my mother's contempt.

'Stout in a chair arm,' said Dad, 'whose cockeyed idea was that?'

What Aunty Myra thinks is not recorded. Not much, I would guess, as she's more taken up with her own gifts than anything given to her. Grandma, who has been quite happy with the old sossed-down chair this new Utility article has superseded, now takes it over as it's quite low and handy for sitting in front of the kitchen range with the toasting fork, or reading the *Evening Post* while she waits for her bread to bake, and it is in this chair she sits in recollection all through my childhood.

Meanwhile Aunty Myra blitzes the family with presents. Returning from India on HMS *Northway* in 1946, she brings with her all the spoils of the East. Even her suitcases are souvenirs. ('Natural pigskin, Walter. Hand stitched. I knocked him right down.') There are shawls, tray-cloths and no end of embroidery. ('All hand-done, Lilian. It's so intricate they go blind doing it, apparently. Just sat there in the street.') We are presented with a blood-red Buddha. ('I don't care if it is a God,' said Mam when we get it home, 'I am not having it on the sideboard with a belly-button that size.') The Buddha is just the tip of the iceberg and Myra regales us with gifts, very few of which we want; there are paper knives for the letters we seldom get, grotesquely carved salad servers for the salad we seldom serve, table mats, napkin rings, yet more accoutrements of that civilised life we never manage to lead, and so doomed to be consigned in due course to the bottom of the wardrobe and eventual wuthering by Dad.

There are also, as Dad puts it, 'cartloads of photographs',

all neatly pasted up and labelled in a clutch of albums that pose a new boredom hazard.

'Don't let's get landed with the photographs,' Dad would warn as we trail up from Tong Road, but since they are invariably on hand to flesh out some anecdote of her military career that Aunty Myra is anxious to recount there is seldom any escape.

We soon become familiar with the sights of Bombay, Calcutta and Dehra Dunn. Here is Aunty and colleagues outside the 'WAAF-ery' at the Astoria Hotel; Aunty in a sari on the balcony of the YMCA; Aunty at the Taj Mahal; and photos of the entire staff of 305 Maintenance Unit gathered for Kiplingesque occasions like 'The Farewell to Wilson Barse'.

I am twelve when I first see these albums, which duly take their place, along with other family relics, in the sitting-room dresser in which, while Grandma is dozing in the kitchen, I do my customary Saturday afternoon 'rooting'. One of the albums in particular fascinates me (and even today it falls open at the place): it has a photo, postcard size, of two Australian soldiers, 'Jordy' and 'Ossie', standing in bush hats and bathing trunks against a background of palm trees. 'Jordy' is unremarkable, with a lascivious other-ranks sort of face. It is 'Ossie' who draws the eye, better-looking, with his arms folded and smiling, and with some reason, as he is weighed down, practically over-balanced, by what, even in the less than skimpy bathing trunks of the time, is a dick of enormous proportions,

Jordy and Ossie

the bathing costume in effect just a hammock in which is lolling this colossal member. Underneath Aunty has written, roguishly:

'Yes, girls! It's all real!'

At some point, in deference I imagine to Grandma's sensibilities ('Nay, Myra'), this caption has been scratched out. Or perhaps it is an act of prudent censorship before Aunty's marriage a year or two later. This takes her back into the RAF as her husband is a regular aircraftman, and henceforth her life is spent shuttling between bases in Singapore and Hong Kong and Kuala Lumpur.

Stan, Myra's husband, is ten years younger than she is, though to my adolescent eyes there doesn't seem much difference between them. Shortly after they are married we go to Grandma's for Christmas high tea. Meals at Gilpin Place are at the customary hour, dinner at noon, high tea around six, with a cup of tea and 'something to finish off with' around nine. Christmas, though, was harder to accommodate to this routine, though not at our house, where 'Dad has to watch his stomach and it doesn't do for him to wait', so with us the turkey would go in the night before, the smell of Christmas morning that of the turkey already cooked and waiting to be put on the table prompt at twelve.

This particular Christmas arrangements at Grandma's are in chaos. Our arrival is always deliberately timed to avoid the King's Speech, as both Myra and Kathleen are fervent patriots. A (literally) standing joke at Christmas is how to avoid being in the room when Aunty Kath jumps to her feet at the first note of the National Anthem – a reverent stance, head bowed, hands clasped, which Dad has been imitating at home for weeks beforehand.

The King's Speech is always a bit of a cliffhanger on account of his stutter, the conversation afterwards generally on the lines of 'How well he does, considering . . .' Having sidestepped all that, we arrive this year around four to find Grandma and Aunty Kath still clearing up after Christmas dinner, which has had to be put back because the newly-weds have been so late getting up. They have now retired upstairs again 'for a nap' so that high tea at six seems unlikely. It is scheduled for seven, but seven comes and then eight and still the middle-aged lovers have not come down. Aunt Eveline has gone through her entire repertoire twice, starting with 'Glamorous Night' and ending with 'Bless This

House'. Dad dutifully accompanies her, with Mam urging him in view of his duodenal to 'have a biting-on', i.e. a snack.

I am thirteen or fourteen at this time but the significance of this elongated siesta is lost on me, as I keep asking why someone can't just go upstairs and wake them up.

'Nay, Alan,' Dad says with withering contempt, though had I shown any awareness of what was going on that would probably have earned his contempt too, sex with Dad always a difficult area. My brother presumably knows, but he has the sense to say nothing. Grandma is embarrassed by the whole business and it's only Aunty Kathleen, always having taken a vicarious pleasure in her younger sister's life, who plainly finds it highly exciting.

When, around nine, the two of them do eventually come downstairs it's not at all shamefacedly, though the meal has to be eaten hurriedly and with some strain, because no sooner is it over than we have to rush to catch the last tram from City Square back up to Headingley, with the ageing lovers, still famished for sex, going straight back upstairs.

As we grow up Aunty Myra in particular tries to stake more of a claim in both of us. That Gordon has chosen to go into the RAF for his National Service and, as Mam puts it, 'passed for a pilot' puts him firmly in Aunty Myra's territory, enabling her to have long discussions about RAF billets and postings in a jargon from which we are naturally excluded. 'Well,' says Mam resignedly, 'she was always a big Gordon fan.'

Even with me, 'the clever one', she tends to lasso my accomplishments to her, 'You get your brains from me' the crudest form of it, a claim never made for themselves by Mam or Dad, who didn't know where my brains came from and didn't much care either.

'Look, Walt,' said Aunty Myra, standing with Dad at the barrier in City Square waiting for a tram, 'just look at that girl with a wealth of auburn hair,' the 'wealth' and the 'auburn' both designed to impress Dad with the sensitivity of her observation and the breadth of her vocabulary, whereas all it did was depress him with the folly of her social pretension. But the phrase lives on and becomes another family joke.

In retrospect these disparagements seem petty and mean-minded, the aunties' splashy behaviour an occasion for fun and reminiscence now as it became a family joke then. For

Dad, though, these disparagements are defensive, the response of a mild and unassertive man who feels such self-advertisement calls many of his innate assumptions into question. These are his wife's sisters, after all, but his wife is not like this, nor, if he can help it, are his children going to be. Showing off as a child, I often made him cringe, and though he never says it he probably thinks that that is my aunties 'coming out' in me and that Aunty Myra is right, I do take after them.

As I grow older I come to judge them myself from much the same standpoint as Mam and Dad, as embarrassed as Dad was by their pretensions, as mindful as Mam that it was the pair of them ('Well, you get it from both sides') who had made her so timid.

Still, as I see now, pretension takes pluck and both the aunties took on the world as Mam and Dad never quite did, somewhere finding the confidence to sail through life without being put down.

'Well, they have a lot off,' Mam would say.

So, despite the outside lav and the sheaf of newspapers hung behind the lav door, the bucket under the sink for the tea leaves and slops and (when caught short) pee, and the drizzle of soot from the railway notwithstanding, they yet contrived to think themselves a cut above the rest, their street a better street, their house a better house. ('Well, it's the end house, that's the difference.')

And so, hieratically vested in their cherished garments ('my little green costume', 'my fawn swagger coat', 'my Persian lamb with the fur bootees') and tricked out in bangles and brooches, bright lipstick and saucy little hats, smiling, as they fondly thought, vivaciously they would step out along those mean gas-smelling streets to catch a tram en route for the pictures at the Assembly Rooms or a dance at the Clock, making a little drama out of a trip to Harehills or a scene in the queue at the Crown. Generally genteel but vulgar if need be, they were sentimental, and with pluck and cheek besides, which if not quite virtues are not unconnected with courage.

Hung up in the back bedroom at Gilpin Place, Aunty Kathleen's shop assistant's black frock is slack and shiny, the pads under the arms stained and smelling of long-dead 4711. She is well into her forties now, cheerful, toothy but not, it is thought, likely to 'get off'. And how can she 'get off', since she has to look after Grandma? But in Manfield's 'on the floor', she still seems a commanding figure, the call 'Miss Peel!' implying a dignity and a rank, the 'Miss' giving her a status that 'Mrs' never quite gives to Mam.

As we grow older and begin to make our way, my brother and I both start to figure more in her conversation. Round-hay ladies wanting court shoes find themselves given an unsought bulletin on 'my nephew in Canada, a pilot in the RAF . . . does that feel easier, madam? . . . My other nephew's just won a scholarship to Oxford . . . Madam has a narrow foot, I'll see if we have something smaller.'

In another respect, too, I do my aunties an injustice. Starved though their lives are of drama, and ready on the thinnest excuse to see themselves in an interesting or tragic light, neither of them at any point indulges this taste for the theatrical by referring even obliquely to the biggest drama that can ever have happened to them, the suicide of their father. There is never the smallest hint of a secret sadness or of a tale that might be told. Loving mystery, in this regard they forgo it entirely. Their father died of a heart attack, here on the kitchen floor, and the conversation does not miss a beat. Though now I see this subterfuge as futile, mistaken, and the lie needless, there is no denying they carry it off superbly; the performances are impeccable. For Grandma and for my parents this is to be expected: to them reticence is second nature. For the aunties, though, not to tell the tale must always have been a sacrifice, and it's a measure of the disgrace attaching to the act that dwelling on it is thought to bring not sympathy but shame. And I see that, in this at least, we have been a united family.

With Myra and husband Stan back on the outskirts of Empire, life returns to its old ways. And there are musical evenings still at Gilpin Place, and Aunt Eveline comes over from Bradford, though now she plays medleys from *Bless the Bride* and *Oklahoma!* and Uncle George sings 'Oh What a Beautiful Morning' as well as 'Bless This House'.

But Grandma is not well, and sitting in the kitchen in the chair that had been bought against Aunty Myra's return she finds the cushion soaked in blood.

Dr Slaney is summoned, the Wolseley parked outside, and he and Aunty Kathleen in her best 'Miss Peel' manner have a hushed conversation in the sitting room. Briefly in hospital, Grandma comes home to the front bedroom at Gilpin Place, where the commode has been brought down from the attic and a fire lit in the tiny grate. She does not read or have the wireless on, but just lies there through the darkening days in that slum bedroom in Wortley, as behind the house the trains are shunted into Holbeck sidings and she waits for what is to come.

Grandma's death in 1950 takes us up to the grave in new Wortley Cemetery where, with St Bartholomew's on one side and Armley Gaol on the other, Grandad Peel had been buried. The grave is unmarked and has always been hard to find, the simple grass-covered mound so plain it seems almost prehistoric ('tump' would describe it), this raised mound the inverted shape of the long zinc baths some houses in Wortley still had hanging outside their back doors.

There is no stone, the only certain identification the withered remains of the flowers taken on our previous visit. This we know was Grandad's grave but that it is the grave of a suicide neither my brother nor I know, though that presumably is why it is unmarked. Putting flowers on it and occasionally on the more elaborate, marble-kerbed pebbled patch belonging to Grandad Bennett is one of the ways of passing Saturday afternoons, which we always spend at Grandma's. One of us threads our way across the cemetery with a jam jar, fills it at the cistern by the wall and bears it brimming back for the vase Mam has brought for the anemones. Sometimes we cut the grass with a pair of inadequate scissors.

Now the grave is open, the sides covered in the same green raffia matting Sleights the greengrocer's have in their window. The coffin being lowered into the hole has up to an hour ago been in the sitting room at Gilpin Place, and with the lid off so the mourners could be taken through by the aunties. ('Would you like to see her?') Dad, predictably, has refused but I am taken in, Kathleen and Myra stroking and kissing Grandma's impassive face. ('Doesn't she look beautiful, Alan?') I have never seen a dead person before, and though I've loved Grandma and liked her I find myself unable to cry or even be moved particularly, just feeling that with the quilted surround and the wimpled face she'd somehow found her way into a chocolate box.

Pretension, though, persists to the end, because as the coffin goes down one sees on the lid that Grandma is said to have died 'in her eightieth year'. This is strictly true as she was seventy-nine, but it doesn't escape what these days would be called Dad's shit-detector.

Nearly thirty years later I find myself filming just outside the gates of the cemetery, the location chosen without reference to me and entirely by chance because it provides a useful cul-de-sac with no passing traffic. In the lunch break I go looking for Grandma's (and Grandad's) grave. But the cemetery has long since been filled up and subsequently landscaped. There are lawns and seats and down-and-outs sleeping on them, together with rubbish and condoms and all the adornments of urban rurality. There are some graves, artfully disposed as features in the landscaping, but there is no grave of ours. Hard to find when I was a boy, now it has gone completely. Still overlooking the cemetery, though, are the black battlements of Armley Gaol. People are no longer buried in the cemetery, which is now a park; but the gaol is ever a gaol and men are still being buried there.

Regularly posted to the Far East, Hong Kong, Singapore, Kuala Lumpur, Aunty Myra resumes with delight the life she has tasted briefly during the war. Though husband Stan is only a warrant officer, now in the twilight of Empire they are entitled to amahs and houseboys and a standard of life way beyond anything they can ever have dreamed of down Tong Road. There are mess dances under the tropic night, beach parties on palm-fringed sands, trips up country and out to the islands, all the time waited on hand and foot by servants who, she is at pains to emphasise, adore her. These postings produce more sheaves of photographs, Aunty M. arm in arm with the devoted servants, beaming on balconies overlooking Hong Kong harbour or days out at Kowloon with Aunty holding armfuls of doubtful Chinese children, a resigned mother looking on.

Because it is children that she has always wanted and never had, believing herself more suited to their upbringing than my mother can ever be and wont to lay claim to a special understanding of their needs, though never grasping how much I certainly want to be left to myself, the fierceness of her regard, the ardour of her attention always making me cringe as a child.

In the intervals of service abroad this lately married couple are posted round England to what is even then only the scattered remnants of the defence establishment. They are stationed at Hednesford, Manston, Padgate or West Malling, airfields where one seldom sees a plane apart from the ceremonial Spitfire marooned among flower beds by the guardhouse, a reminder of the great days when all that stood between the nation and its doom was the RAF.

Now the graceful trees of what was once a grand estate shelter Nissen huts and mean system-built houses where the paths are edged with whitewashed stones and the flowers look ready to stand by their beds. It's a suburb that's not quite a suburb, but billets and married quarters and an environment I feel faintly threatening from the days of my National Service, as if I could still be put to weed these beds and bull the kerbs as once I'd had to do in the army.

In a succession of these allotted accommodations Aunty Myra sets out the souvenirs of their tours overseas – an inlaid chest from Bombay, a nest of tables from Madras; there are bowls from Malaya, linen from Singapore and a painted scroll from Hong Kong. 'The writing means a blessing on this house. They do it while you wait. The boy who did it was crippled but he had a lovely face. Mind you, they're so poor they often cripple them themselves to make them more appealing.' Then Stan, her warrant officer husband, parks me in one of the bamboo armchairs and plies me with earnest questions about what I am doing at Oxford and what I am going to do with my medieval history afterwards. What use is it?

Stan being ten years younger than his wife, she naturally expects him to outlive her. But in 1964 he is flown home from Malaya suffering from inoperable cancer. He is taken first to the RAF Chest Unit which is part of the King Edward VII Hospital for Officers at Midhurst, a palatial mansion down a long drive flush with rhododendrons, with views across the manicured lawns to Chichester and the South Downs.

'It's a tip-top place,' said Aunty Myra. 'The surgeon looking after him is one of the first in the country,' and she gives me a long dramatised account of how this individual, an Air Vice-Marshal, had actually taken her by the arm and called her Mrs Rogerson before going on to explain the hopelessness of the situation.

My aunties were always like this, adducing a special status and reputation for any doctor assigned to them. 'Refined-looking fellow, has a big house at Alwoodley, his wife wears one of them sheepskin coats' is a version of it that's crept into one or two of my plays, though I don't suppose that on most occasions it is as purely snobbish as I make it appear. Perhaps Aunty Myra feels that attached to her often fanciful ascriptions of excellence and accomplishment is some shred of hope, as being a top man meant that he could defy the coming doom. (In Leeds it would have come out as 'You couldn't do better if he were in the Brotherton Wing'.) But the special smile, the squeeze of the arm, the recognition, so Aunty Myra sees it, of her natural breeding were also part of a desire to be different, to be marked out above the common ruck and to have a tale to tell.

But if in Aunty's eyes the top surgeon's concern singles her out, there is a high price to be paid for the touch of the Air Vice-Marshal's hand; it puts paid to hope, else why would he touch her at all? It also put paid to the rhododendrons, the lawns and that terrace which must once have had a grandstand view of the Battle of Britain. In its stead comes a poky Unit hospital in RAF Uxbridge, where, in more pain and discomfort than he need have had, Stan lengthily dies, the customary reluctance of hospitals to prescribe painkillers compounded in military establishments, I imagine, because part of their patients' profession is to be brave.

Deplorable though the place is as a hospital, I am interested in the camp because Uxbridge was where T. E. Lawrence, under the name of Shaw, had enlisted as an aircraftman in the early twenties, an account of which he gives in *The Mint*. This is 1964 but the corrugated-iron huts look scarcely to have changed, and as I wander about the camp in the intervals of sitting baffled by my uncle's bed there is a touch of 'And did those feet' about it. T. E. Lawrence figures in *Forty Years On*, and I see that literature is of as much moment to me as life, so that the death of this recently acquired and only occasionally encountered uncle doesn't really signify. Driving along the M40 today I still glance along the ridge to the tower of Uxbridge Church, in the shadow of which some of life's bleaker moments were spent. Though not as bleak as his, I hear a reproving voice. But I scarcely know him, with his red face and crinkly receding hair, and as an ex-National Serviceman I'm suspicious of 'a regular', even in something so innocuous and relatively wanting in bull as an RAF Maintenance Unit.

Stan having died on active service, he is entitled to a full military funeral and this, at Aunty's wish, he is duly given. It is thus that I find myself at the crematorium at Ruislip walking behind the RAF band (though trying not to be seen to march or even keep time) and led by an officer with a drawn sword between ranks of airmen presenting arms. It seems a bit excessive if, strictly speaking, appropriate, and I am ashamed by the ceremony and its insincerities to the extent that, far from being a comfort, I can scarcely be civil. I see the whole ceremony, much as Dad does, as a lot of splother, cringing at how unreluctantly Aunty is ready to take the limelight, a lone figure in black standing behind the coffin as the band plays.

'Bad acting' I think it, and grief no excuse, the more it shows the less it means my philosophy then, though I suppose I have come to appreciate how often a husband's funeral is the last chance most wives get to cut even a sombre dash or take the stage alone, and that they are not to be blamed if they get their teeth into it. This is her curtain call too. But though I hope I would feel less harshly towards Myra now than I did then, she was a woman who repelled sympathy. I have never come across grief that is transmuted so readily into anger, with no hint of resignation or philosophy. Though naïvely I am somehow expecting it to be all resignation. Try as I do to be more tolerant and understanding,

I find myself tested by posthumous extravagances, of which the military funeral is one, the scattering of the ashes another.

Why I am chosen to accompany my aunty on this errand is something of a mystery. It's probably because at this date I'm the only one of the immediate family who can drive. Glum, unsympathetic and critical of the histrionic strain that runs through her grief, I make an unsatisfactory and unconsoling companion. 'She's putting it on,' I keep thinking, unmitigated by the thought that perhaps she's entitled to do so.

If as a dramatist I am offended by her bad acting, it's as a discerning tourist and seeker-out of unfrequented spots that I deplore the venue for the scattering. It is Ilkley Moor. For one of the various editions of *Beyond the Fringe* I had written a sketch about someone wanting their ashes scattered on the South Shore at Blackpool on August Bank Holiday; Aunty Myra's choice of venue seems not unlike. But it is Ilkley Moor where Aunty says they had their happiest times, and though I wish their enchantments had been less conventionally located (Bolton Abbey, say, or Fountains) it is to Ilkley Moor I drive her.

Having taken her to the edge of the moor, I don't even get out of the car, mumbling something about her doubtless wanting to be alone at a moment like this. Not that there is much chance of that. It is the first warm day of spring, and all over the chosen segment of moorland holidaymakers are taking the sun, even picnicking as presumably she and Stan had done in the happier times now being ultimately commemorated. It seems sensible to me to convey the urn and its contents to a stretch of heather that is less populous, and I diffidently suggest this. But the location is precise and seemingly sacred – it occurs to me now that sex may have marked the spot – and she is not to be shifted from her grim purpose by a few day-trippers.

In hat and gloves and wholly in black, Aunty cuts a distinctive figure as heedless of the sun-seekers she clambers over the rocks, unloading the contents of the urn as she goes. Prudence might have kept it, like a gas mask, in its cardboard box, but no, she brandishes the urn for all to see, this scattering literally her last fling as a loving wife and not a gesture she is prepared to muffle.

I sink lower and lower in the driving seat as she moves among the stunned sunbathers, shedding her load and heedless of the light breeze that whirls the ashes back in her face. Eventually, the urn emptied, she returns to the car: 'He didn't want to leave me,' she says tearfully, wiping a smut from her coat. It's a line of dialogue I might hesitate to wish onto an invented character on grounds of plausibility. But then I might make my character more plausible too, and certainly kinder than the unwilling, unfeeling chauffeur I am this afternoon, my sullen responses more to be censured than her inauthentic extravagances. What she wants is a decent audience, which is what I am determined not to be. Not for the first time on occasions requiring good manners, I think Gordon would have done it better and to hell with authenticity.

In the few years she has left to live Aunty Myra's life seems fuelled by pure anger – anger at the RAF, who had, as she sees it, taken her husband's life and refused her all but the most minimal pension, anger at fate, God even, that has dealt her this blow, anger at my mother, who has a husband and children and a cushioned life, anger above all at her other sister, Aunty Kathleen.

Kathleen has always in the past been Myra's companion and confidante, and Myra must have assumed that she would remain a lifelong spinster and so be always available for consolation and companionship. But to everyone's surprise, on the eve of her retirement from Manfield's, Kathleen is courted and briskly married by an elderly widower from Australia. It's a turn of events which takes Kathleen as much by surprise as it does everyone else, as her husband, a Mr Roach, is no more romantic than his name, plump, opinionated and small; Aunty Kathleen, never having expected to get married at all, can afford to have a detached view of these shortcomings. Exit Miss Peel; enter Mrs Roach.

The wedding ought to have been, like its predecessors, at St Mary's, Tong Road, but now there is grass growing between the paving stones there and the church like half the neighbourhood is on the brink of demolition. So at some church in Morecambe, where Bill has got them a little bungalow, there is the wedding of Mr William Roach and Miss Kathleen Elizabeth Peel, Aunty Kath flanked by Mam in gloves and 'that little maroon duster coat I had to Gordon's wedding', with Dad looking long-suffering in the back row. Dad dislikes being photographed, and faced with a camera his habitual geniality is replaced by a look of pained discomfort and boredom.

'Don't pull your jib, Dad,' Mam mutters, 'try and look natural.' But it is to no effect and in this mood there is no one he resembles so much as Somerset Maugham in his last days at the Villa Mauresque.

Happily, I do not have to go through this ordeal as I am in New York with *Beyond the Fringe*. Notably absent, too, is Aunty Myra, though she would probably have been looking as pained as Dad had she been on the church steps and not in one of the last outposts of the Empire, Kuala Lumpur

Mam on an outing with Somerset Maugham, 1952

possibly or Singapore. Having married late herself, to find her sister doing the same must have taken some of the shine off her own tardy nuptials. It was never on the cards that Aunty Kathleen would 'land a man', if only because she talks so much.

'I don't know how he managed to shut her up long enough to pop the question,' said Dad, though husband Bill was far from ungarrulous himself. This is one of Aunty Myra's complaints against him, that he talks a lot and that he bores her, but it is not the quality of his conversation that is the real issue: had Aunty Kathleen been marrying Isaiah Berlin it would have made no difference. No. The case against Bill is that he has disrupted the natural order of things.

Aunty Kathleen is the sister who stayed at home to look after her mother, and when that mother died stayed on as such dutiful daughters often did, living in the same house, guardian of the home where Myra and Stan could stay when they came on leave, and where we would still come for the ritual high tea on Christmas Day, though Grandma, who had given it fun and point, was now long since dead. Her death, though, does not change Kathleen's life one bit;

she still works at Manfield's, keeps up with a vast network of friends and correspondents, writes innumerable letters, her job, her style, her way of talking unaltered since she and Myra went out to dances together in the twenties.

Now all that changes. Kathleen sells the house in Gilpin Place, and with it what is left of the grand furniture that came over from Halifax before the First War. Sold for a song is the huge oak kist that occupies the wall of one bedroom, and likewise a fruitwood sideboard the size of an altar, which all my childhood stood in the kitchen that its polished mellow wood reflected. In the little semi-detached bungalow at Bare on the outskirts of Morecambe that they had found for themselves and which backed, as did Gilpin Place, onto a railway, the sideboard would not even have got through the door.

Having followed in her sister's footsteps by making a late marriage, Aunty Kathleen continues the pattern when she and husband Bill take up globetrotting. When Aunty Myra brings her husband home to die, Aunty Kathleen and Bill are about to embark on a world cruise culminating in a visit to her new family in Australia. In the face of Myra's disapproval of both the marriage and the world cruise, it takes courage (plus the determination of her fierce Australian hamster of a husband) to persist. But off they go.

So now it is Kathleen's turn to send home photographs of herself in a rickshaw, or garlanded with flowers after some shipboard dinner dance, posed against the taffrail with Bill in his white dinner jacket, and even, as Myra has done so often, brandishing some Oriental tot while its patient mother looks on. Letters come with hopes of better news of Stan, filled with accounts of their travels, the snaps enclosed. Meanwhile Stan fades and dies, and Aunty Myra crouches over her one-bar electric fire as through the letter box come the postcards of palm trees and koala bears.

Myra lives in a succession of briefly rented rooms, first in Midhurst, then Uxbridge, and finally at West Malling in Kent. These comfortless accommodations and the meals that go with them – or rather don't, as they seldom have cooking facilities, so have to be taken in cheap cafés serving spaghetti on toast or poached egg, tea and bread and butter – exude a particular sort of hopelessness quite separate from the sad circumstances which have brought her to them. Aunty Myra had too many sharp corners to be one of her characters, but they are the setting for many of the novels of Barbara Pym, and one of the reasons I find her books quite lowering to read. Eventually, though, Myra comes back north, choosing, as she thinks anyway, to face old age in a bungalow on a bleak little development at Wharton outside Lytham. Significantly, though this is not mentioned, it's across the road from an airfield.

Most of us, certainly as we get older, prefer it if our lives are played out against a permanent set and with a cast that is largely unaltered; we may change our own role and status (and partner), but it's better if friends and relations (the extras in our drama) remain fixed in their roles and the set-ups to which we have grown accustomed. The death of a close friend or, almost as distasteful, a divorce, alters our landscape; there is a distressing upheaval.

When Aunty Myra married and went abroad she not unreasonably expected that her sister would continue in the part which she had always played, the stay-at-home sister, unmarried and on call. After she'd tasted the joys of marriage with her Mr Roach, I've a feeling Aunty Kathleen may want this also but now it's too late.

Whether her husband wants a wife or not, he certainly

wants a housekeeper, and he makes no secret of his desire to take her back to Australia. In the meantime they sit in their poky semi-detached bungalow by the railway at the back end of Morecambe, while thirty miles down the coast Aunty Myra sits in hers. Occasionally they meet, but the rift is never wholly healed. In a trashy novel, the little Australian would have died . . . and in a murder mystery in dubious circumstances; the sisters would have made it up, and life would have got back to normal, Stan made a saint and the distasteful episode of Kathleen's marriage never referred to. But it wasn't quite as tidy as that.

When it came to bringing comfort to the sick, no one was quicker off the mark than Kathleen or Myra. They both make a beeline for any bedside, the first hint of sickness fetching them round with Lucozade or calf's-foot jelly and a flow of enlivening chatter. Such visits were to be avoided at all costs, and so if there is illness in our family Dad prefers to keep it dark. ('Well, you get weary with them.') Mam's health has not been good for a few months and Aunty Myra has somehow got wind of it, and since she is now a widow she is a looser cannon than she was when married. Sure enough, she insists on coming over to stay.

'For Lilian's sake, Walter. You see,' Aunty Myra said, smiling her Bette Davis smile, 'I understand her.'

It also gives her an opportunity of demonstrating her home-making skills, taking over the cooking and generally playing the model housewife. It takes very little of this to bring about a rapid improvement in my mother's health, and on the night in question she and Dad have gone out to the pictures, leaving Aunty Myra at home with me.

For a while I try and talk to her but her grief, which shows no sign of abating, already bores me, and I am expected to corroborate the intense anger she is still feeling at the untimeliness of her husband's death and the unfeelingness of the RAF. Soon wearying of this I retire to the back room, the junk room as it's always called, where I am labouring over the series of sketches which will eventually turn into *Forty Years On*. While I struggle with this entirely literary piece in one room, in another Aunty Myra enacts a far more vivid scene that could come out of a play by D. H. Lawrence.

Not a reader, and too grief-stricken to want to watch television, Myra seeks solace in housework. The flat in Headingley where we are then living is bright and cosy, and Mam has set out her Staffordshire figures with their maimed hands and broken necks, the supposedly Sheraton table she has picked up at a sale and all the other purchases which make the place 'a bit more classy'. There is nothing to be done with any of these, which Aunty Myra doesn't have much time for anyway. Her concern is the gas oven, an ancient Belling that had come with the flat and clean, so far as a gas oven is ever clean, but not in its inward parts.

Gas ovens can be readily dismantled for ease of cleaning, but ours has never been thus deconstructed until this evening, when Aunty Myra takes it in hand. And yes, it is to sublimate her grief and perhaps to help with the running of the household, but another interpretation is possible, having to do with Aunty Myra's superiority as a housewife and as a forces wife at that, one who knows how to keep a kitchen spotless and has had amahs and dhobi boys to do it. Now it is our turn, and while I labour in the back room our gas stove is split into its component parts and spread over the kitchen floor.

Unsurprisingly, the grease is caked on and proves more intractable than she had thought. In her scheme of things, of course, it would never have been allowed to get into such a state. She would have cleaned it – or supervised the cleaning of it – every week. So when in due course Mam and Dad return from the pictures it is to find Aunty Myra still sitting on the kitchen floor with the gas oven still unresolved around her.

Dad seldom loses his temper, and had I had to put words into his mouth I would have expected him only to say, 'Nay, Myra, what's all this?' But I had forgotten how such a ludicrous incident fitted into the undeclared war between the sisters, with Mam always portrayed as the silly, inefficient, unworldly one and Myra the new model housewife. There were tears from both sisters and, almost unheard of, shouting from my father, before all parties went to bed, the oven left in disarray.

To clean down in another woman's house, while ostensibly doing her a favour, is also to do her an injury and a disservice. Mam is house-proud but her pride begins with her little walnut work-box, her green glass doorstop and her blue and white plates. It doesn't extend to the dark recesses behind the Belling or the space between the top cupboard and the ceiling, the kind of areas only a sergeant major doing a kit inspection would ever dream of investigating.

But Aunty Myra has spent her life in camps where such

fastidious probings were the norm, camps where whitened stones led up to the gates and where the formations on the square are echoed in the open order of the flowers in their beds. She has spent her evenings pressing her husband's uniform, blancoing his belt and even bulling his boots. Now he is dead she cleans the gas oven almost as an act of piety; she is doing what she has always done (or seen to be done) in his memory. None of this, of course, is appreciated by Mam and least of all by Dad and, bereaved or not, Myra leaves the next morning, the seriousness of this absurd incident reflected in the fact that it never becomes a family joke.

In the event Myra does not long survive her husband, her sojourn in her cold little bungalow bringing on pneumonia. She has so often contrasted her lonely situation and her toughness of spirit with my mother's more cosseted existence that at first I refuse to believe she is ill, taking it to be some sort of sideshow staged to divert attention from my mother, who has just come out of hospital after her first bout of depression. It's only when her letters start coming from the infirmary in Blackpool that I grudgingly acknowledge that there must be something in it. Dad has been similarly sceptical and it is only my brother, who has always felt less unkindly towards her, who takes it entirely seriously. Even so it is not at all plain what the matter is, the doctor diagnosing some sort of asthma, a condition from which she has never suffered.

So her death when it comes takes me by surprise. My brother telephones from the hospital, and I am in the middle of saying that even so I don't think it is as serious as all that when he tells me she has died. My parents had been at her bedside when she had taken my father's hand, scrabbling at her wrist to indicate he must have her watch. So Dad, who has always found her a difficult woman, is now as plagued with remorse as I am.

So entrenched, though, are my convictions about her character that even when she is in the grave it does not entirely undercut them, so that I catch myself feeling that her death was somehow not quite *sincere*: she had died just for effect. Aunty Kathleen keeps saying that she had never recovered from the death of her husband and that she has died of a broken heart. Ordinarily I would have made a joke of this, taken it as just another instance of the aunties' pretentiousness. But now I keep my thoughts to myself and Dad does too.

The funeral is at a featureless crematorium in Lytham St Annes. Afterwards we go for lunch to a roadhouse on the outskirts. I sit next to my grandmother's niece, Cousin Florence, who keeps a boarding house in Blackpool. A down-to-earth woman, she eats a large meal of lukewarm lasagne, then puts down her knife and fork and says, 'Well, that's the first time I've dined off brown plates.' Grief is not much in evidence, though with Cousin Florence it is hardly to be expected. Her husband's name was Frank, and six months before we had had a two-page letter filling us in on all her news. Halfway down the second page came the sentence: 'Frank died last week, haven't we been having some weather?' Seldom can a comma have borne such a burden.

In the bungalow that November afternoon, huddled in their coats against the cold that had killed their sister, Mam and Aunty Kathleen divide her possessions between them. Many of them are in tea chests from Singapore that have not been opened since she and her dying husband came back two years before. There are sheaves of tablecloths, bundles of napkins, sets of sheets and pillow-cases, all of them stored up against the day when she and Stan would cease their globetrotting and settle down. Most of the linen has never been used, the cutlery still in its tissue paper. At one point Mam speaks up for a set of steak knives with bone handles, evidence that she is still dreaming of her own life being transformed and that she might one day branch out. They are still in their tissue paper twenty-five years later when she herself dies.

There are few family heirlooms. Mam gets Grandma's yew Windsor chair, which she has always wanted and which she partly credits with setting her off liking 'nice things'. I bag two pairs of steel shears that had been used to cut lino and oilcloth in Grandpa Peel's hardware shop in Union Street, West Vale; fine, sensible objects shaped to fit the hand so that they are a physical pleasure to use, and come in handy for cutting paper. Back in 1966 I want them because they have a history which is also my history; but also because they are the kind of thing a writer has on his table. And they are on my table now as I write, the tools of my trade as they were the tools of my great grandfather's. Cut, cut, cut.

Though I do not speak up for them, it must have been then that Aunty Myra's photograph albums are given over to me on the assumption that, since I am the educated one, I should keep the family record, or a censored version of it as Grandad Peel's suicide is not yet out in the open. Still, there in the album is Ossie, lazily grinning on his tropical beach, the great sag of his dick as astonishing now as it had been when I was a boy, the page still scuffed where Aunty Myra had expunged her first roguish caption.

This sharing-out is a bizarre occasion, a kind of Christmas with endless presents to open, Mam and Aunty Kathleen by turns shrieking with laughter and then in floods of tears. Neither of them wants for much now; both have tea towels and sheets to last them all their days with tray cloths and napkins in their own bottom drawers that they are never going to use either. And more than the funeral itself or the bitter cold that grips the bungalow, it is this redundancy of possessions that makes them think of death.

Conscious that I have done Aunty Myra an injustice but knowing, too, that I would do exactly the same again, I try and write about her in my diary:

She was a great maker of lists/inventories/lists of friends/lists of expenses/shopping lists/records of meter readings/contents of cases. It was a habit acquired in the Equipment Wing of RAF Innsworth, ticking off kit on lists on clipboards; lists of property which grew with every posting as she moved with her husband from station to station, and quarters to quarters. What is yours is what is signed for, and what is signed for must one day be accounted for, so a list must be made. And a check list in case the first list is lost. These are my possessions. I own these. I have these signatures.

On the day of her husband's death, she signed for his property: for the watch that still ticked on the dead wrist, the ring loose on the finger, the pyjamas in which he lay.

And when he was dead two years, and she was in a bungalow on the outskirts of nowhere in particular, she was still making lists: guy ropes for a life that didn't have much point, evidence of what she had and therefore what she was, and a sign that she was not settled there either, that soon she would up sticks and off. We found the lists, the packing cases still unopened: tea sets from Hong Kong, Pyrex won in raffles in a sergeants' mess in Kowloon in 1947, the sewing of amahs, the pictures of house-boys, her husband's uniform, his best BD and belt, all piled up in the back room of a bungalow on the outskirts of Lytham St Annes.

～

Aunty Kathleen holds up a pair of her husband's pyjama bottoms.

'See, Lilian,' she giggles, 'look at his little legs.' They are in the front bedroom at Morecambe while in the kitchen Bill, the husband in question, fills Dad in on the ins and outs of sanitary engineering in Western Australia.

It is Christmas Day early in the seventies, and Mam and Dad and me have driven over from home to the cheerless bungalow in Bare for Christmas dinner, a last faint echo of those communal gatherings twenty-odd years before. But now there is no Aunt Eveline to play the piano or Uncle George to sing, just this oddly married couple, half-strangers to one another still, a marriage of mutual convenience meant to keep one another company in their declining years.

With her regular gifts of shoe-trees Aunty Kath had hitherto held the record for boring Christmas presents, but Bill shows he is no slouch in this department either when he presents me with the history of some agricultural college in New South Wales (second volume only).

'You did history, Alan. This should interest you.' He has served in the First War and we spend much of Christmas afternoon leafing through the pages while he points out the names of the sons and grandsons of men in 'his mob' who have done time studying agriculture.

Quite what he is doing is England is not plain as he seldom misses an opportunity of running it down, along with blacks, Jews and, when Mam and Aunty Kathleen are out of the room, women generally. Dad, who has never enrolled in the sex war, lapses into Somerset Maugham mode, his face a picture of boredom and misery until the time comes when we can make our farewells and thankfully head off home in the Mini. Mam now tells us about the pyjama incident and becomes helpless with laughter, the mitigating 'But she's very good-hearted' which is always tacked onto any gossip involving Aunty Kathleen hard to employ where her husband is concerned, as good-hearted Bill plainly isn't.

Considering Morecambe is only three-quarters of an hour away from the village, Mam and Dad see the old newly marrieds relatively seldom as they are often abroad on trips, life in the bungalow by the railway enlivened by a visit to Switzerland, for instance, and a lengthy Pacific cruise culminating in a visit to Australia to meet her husband's family. It is tacitly assumed that this must be a prelude to them upping sticks and settling down there, but nothing is said. Instead, they come back and resume their life at Bare, slightly to Dad's dismay as it inevitably means more slides with Bill in his flowered shorts, Aunty Kathleen in a sarong; one way and another we'd been looking at pictures like this for nearly thirty years.

Scarcely, though, are they back from this odyssey when something begins to happen in Aunty Kathleen's head. She has always been intensely sociable, still with many friends in Leeds, and much of her time, home or away, is spent in keeping up with what she calls 'her correspondence' – scores of letters regularly fired off to friends and acquaintances, few of them of course known to her hubby, whom she may even press into running her over to Leeds to see them.

'I've half a dozen people who're always begging me to pop in,' says Miss Prothero, 'one of them a chiropodist.' A character in an early play, hers is the unmistakable voice of Aunty Kath.

At some point, though, after their return from Australia her address book goes missing and with it half her life. Without this roster of names and addresses she is cut adrift. Mam doesn't think the address book has been lost at all and that Bill, in an effort to loosen her grip on the past and make sure she settles first in Morecambe, and eventually Australia, has himself deliberately mislaid this handbook to sociability.

True or not the effect is disastrous. Out of touch with her convoy of friends and acquaintances, she begins to drift aimlessly. Her discourse becomes wayward and Bill, who has several times remarked to Dad on how all the sisters could gab, now finds that her utterance accelerates, becomes garbled and impossible to follow. It doesn't take much of this before he commits her to a mental hospital, which is Lancaster Moor again. Indeed she is briefly in the same ward as Mam had been on her first admission a few years before, and there comes a time when Mam is in the psychiatric wing at Airedale Hospital and her sister in a similar wing at Lancaster.

Misconceiving where my father's loyalties lie, the little Australian makes no attempt at fellow-feeling, attributing both their misfortunes to the Peel family. Unsurprisingly Dad will have none of it; Mam's plight is not the same as her sister's, and that he might be thought to have anything in common with his coarse conceited brother-in-law is not even a joke.

Insofar as her condition is diagnosed at all, Kathleen is said to be suffering from arteriosclerosis of the brain: in a word, dementia. The catch-all term nowadays is Alzheimer's but that didn't have quite the same currency in the early seventies, or its current high profile. Insofar as it was futile to tell Aunty Kathleen anything and expect her to remember it for more than a moment, her condition was like that of an Alzheimer's patient, but the manner of her deterioration is not so simple as a mere forgetting. Not for her a listless, dull-eyed wordless decline; with her it is all rush, gabble, celerity.

She had always been a talker but now her dementia unleashes torrents of speech, monologues of continuous anecdote and dizzying complexity, one train of thought switching to another without signal or pause, rattling across points and through junctions at a rate no listener can follow.

Her speech, so imitable in the past, becomes impossible to reproduce, though now taking myself seriously as a writer and praised for 'an ear for dialogue' I dutifully try, making notes of these flights of speech as best I can, then when I get home trying to set them down but without success.

Embarking on one story, she switches almost instantly to another and then another, and while her sentences still retain grammatical form they have no sequence or sense. Words pour out of her as they always have and with the same vivacity and hunger for your attention. But to listen to they are utterly bewildering, following the sense like trying to track a particular ripple in a pelting torrent of talk.

Still, despite this formless spate of loquacity she remains recognisably herself, discernible in the flood those immutable gentilities and components of her talk which have always characterised her (and been such a joke). 'If you follow me, Lilian . . .', 'As it transpired, Walter . . .', 'Ready to wend my way, if you take my meaning . . .' So that now, with no story to tell (or half a dozen), she must needs still tell it as genteelly as she has ever done but at five times the speed, her old worn politenesses detached from any narrative but still whole and hers, bobbing about in a ceaseless flood of unmeaning; demented, as she herself might have said, but very nicely spoken.

And as with her speech, so it is with her behaviour. Surrounded by the senile and by the wrecks of women as hopelessly, though differently, demented as she is, she still clings to the notion that she is somehow different and superior. Corseted in her immutable gentilities she still contrives to make something special out of her situation and her role in it.

'He'll always give me a smile,' she says of an impassive nurse who is handing out the tea. 'I'm his favourite.'

'This is my chair. They'll always put me here because this corner's that bit more select.'

Her life has been made meaningful by frail, fabricated connections, and now, when the proper connections in her brain are beginning to break down, it is this flimsy tissue of social niceties that still holds firm.

In this demented barracks she remains genteel, in circumstances where gentility is hardly appropriate: a man is wetting himself; a woman is howling.

'I'll just have a meander down,' says Aunty, stepping round the widening pool of piss. 'They've stood me in good stead, these shoes.'

The setting for this headlong fall from sense is the long-stay wing of the hospital: it's a nineteenth-century building, a fairly spectacular one at that, and in any other circumstances one might take pleasure in it as an example of the picturesque, in particular the vast Gothic hall which, with its few scattered figures, could be out of an Ackermann print. But the scattered figures are shaking with dementia or sunk in stupor and depression; it is Gothic, but the Gothic, too, of horror, madness and despair.

Of these surroundings Kathleen seems unaware, though her eyes sometimes fill with tears in a distress that cannot settle on its object, and should a nurse come by it is straightaway replaced by the beaming smile, refined voice and all the trappings of the old Miss Peel. But the grimness of the institution, the plight of the patients and Kathleen's immunity to sense make her a distressing person to visit, and Dad is naturally reluctant to take Mam lest she sees her sister's condition as in any way reflecting her own. But when Mam is well enough and freed from her depression they go over to Lancaster regularly and conscientiously, and probably see more of Kathleen mad then they had lately seen of her sane.

She was never so touching as now when her brain is beginning to unravel.

'Give us a kiss, love,' she says when I am going. 'That's one thing I do like.' Then, as a nurse passes, 'Hello! Do you know my mother-in-law?' She smiles her toothy smiles as if this were just a slip of the tongue. 'No. I mean my father.' And she gives me another kiss.

Now, though, it is the summer of 1974. Mam is in and out of Airedale Hospital, Dad driving daily backwards and forwards in the loving routine that eventually, early in August, kills him.

It is perhaps because I am now forty, and am unappealingly conscious that the death of a father is one of the great unrepeatables and ought, if I am a proper writer, to be recorded, that about this time I begin to keep a more systematic diary, through which much of the rest of Aunty Kathleen's story can be told.

Sunday, 1 September 1974, Yorkshire. Drive down to Airedale to see Mam. For a while we sit outside in the hot sheltered sunshine, then go indoors and talk to another patient, Mary, who has been in hospital with Mam once before. Mam is more rational, slow and a bit distanced but collected, though able to talk more easily to Mary than to me. I drive back home and the telephone is going just as I am putting the key in the door and it's Gordon, who's ringing to say he's on his way north.

What has happened is that Aunty Kathleen has disappeared from Lancaster Moor, walking out of the ward in her summer frock last Wednesday afternoon and not having been seen since. The police begin looking on Thursday but find no trace of her. Now Gordon feels he must come up to search for her himself, and also to talk to her husband to see whether he can throw any light on her disappearance. He thinks he ought to visit her old haunts and suggests to me possible places where she might be, friends she might have gone to in Leeds, Morecambe and even Scarborough. This is someone who is incapable of keeping her mind or her discourse in one channel for more than ten seconds together, so I get slightly cross at these suggestions and try and persuade him not to come. I think I've succeeded and it's a relief when I can get the phone down, have a bath and go up to Dubb Syke for my supper.

When I get back around midnight it's to find Gordon waiting. There have been no further developments, except that the police seem to have been half-hearted in their searching, saying that with three mental hospitals in Lancaster disappearances are relatively common. I feel guilty that I have no feelings about it, but my case is that if Aunty Kathleen has had the wit to get any distance or to find someone to stay with then she should be left alone. Besides, if she is dead then she is probably better off. And if she is half-dead of exposure or whatever I am not sure that I would want to authorise desperate resuscitation measures to bring her round and put her back in that dismal fortress of a hospital. But in the night I hear the rain tippling down and think of her lying under a bush somewhere, bewildered as a child.

Monday, 2 September 1974. I work in the morning, then drive over to Lancaster to meet Gordon, who has been walking round fields and barns and a cemetery but found nothing. He has shown Aunty's photograph to bus conductors, as someone thinks she may have been seen on a bus. He has been to the hospital and talked to the orderlies, who do not think she can have gone far as she got into a panic if she thought she was going on a journey. One of the more lucid patients thinks she may have seen her getting into a Mini, and this raises the question whether Bill, who has a Mini, may have abducted her. When told of her disappearance he has said to the police, 'She will be found in water.'

This suggests that he had been told of the drowning of her father; the fact that such a recent recruit to the family should have been so readily told a secret that had been kept from us for forty years making me slightly resentful.

The thought, though, that her husband might have something to do with her disappearance is chilling, the more so since it's known he is anxious to get back to Australia but does not have the money to do so and (though this is unverified) does not have the disposal of what money Kathleen may have left; not much, I imagine, but maybe just enough. The police are not interested in any of this; to them it is just another disappearance.

Exhausted we drive back over the Pennines to Airedale to see Mam who is more rational than yesterday, discussing a little what is to happen when she comes out of hospital. Tomorrow Gordon goes to see Bill. A policewoman called at the bungalow and found on his door a notice saying 'Knock at your peril'. He had mentioned his Australian plans but then shut up about them quickly.

Unrecorded in my diary are the details of Gordon's visit to the bungalow in Bare, where he had in effect to ask Aunty Kathleen's husband whether he had done away with his wife. This is, to say the least, a difficult assignment and I could see no way of accomplishing it. But my brother, always more conscientious than I am, and anxious to do the right thing even when it might not be the right thing to do, feels he must make the attempt.

He gets nowhere of course but at least comes away convinced that Bill no more knows the whereabouts of Aunty Kathleen than we do. There is, though, a certain shiftiness about him, perhaps because, with his wife irretrievably demented, he may have decided to give her up as a bad job and decamp to Australia. But that is a different thing.

We enquire again whether she has been seen at the bus station, another dutiful but futile exercise; she can no longer have known what a bus was, let alone where it might be stationed. Capable of catching a bus she would not have been in hospital in the first place.

Tuesday, 3 September 1974. First we search on the other side of the road where the hospital borders the prison, two total institutions that blend seamlessly into one another with no evidence from the atmosphere or the architecture which is prison, which is hospital. We look in a long dyke bordering a rubbish dump, high in nettles.

There are broken bits of surgical equipment, lavatory pans and big juicy evil-looking blackberries and the tall mulleins that grow in our own garden. We follow the filthy stream that runs along the bottom and come to furnace rooms and a smoking dump. A furnace man speaks out of the depths of a hut. Then there are nurses in clean rooms by a smooth lawn. We come back, Gordon saying that we would give it up soon but could we walk down the cinder track by Aunty's ward which leads eventually to the river? I think it pointless and am cross and ill-tempered because I want my lunch and it all seems so useless; in such surroundings she could be two feet away and we would not see her. But we go on looking and it's about half past one that we find her.

The wood runs from the cinder track to the edge of the motorway. I get over the wall into the wood a little way up the field, which has been newly sown with some winter crop. Gordon is ahead of me somewhere but I lose him when I get over the wall and start blundering about the wood. Someone has been here already as I can see the bracken and brambles trampled down, the police probably with their dogs, searching. Looking back on it now it seems as if I knew I must go to the end of the wood last, and only search by the wall at the finish. So I work along the hedge that borders the next field where I see now that Gordon is. Then I turn up towards the end of the wood where there seems to be a break in the wall which must lead up to the verge of the M6. The wood is full of terrible noise, the din of lorries passing, the traffic thundering ceaselessly by shaking the trees. I go towards the break in the wall and then I see her.

I see her legs. One red sandal off. Her summer frock. Her bright white hair, and if I look closely I think there is the yellow flesh of her face. She is lying face downwards, one arm stretched out. I stand there doing nothing with a mixture of feelings. Revulsion at this dead thing, which I do not want to look at closely. Exultation that I have found her and, shockingly, pleasure that it is me who has found her who had thought the whole search futile. But there is wonder, too, at the providence that has led us to this spot among the drenched undergrowth, the whole place heaving with noise, nature and not nature.

I go back through the wood a little and shout 'Gordon, Gordon' again and again. I must have shouted it twenty times until once the call happens to come in a break in the traffic, and he comes across from the field. He bends over her, touches the body as I have failed to do and says 'Such a little thing', and he puts his hand over his face. He says he thinks her nose has been bleeding. I see her outstretched arm, mushroom white, the flesh shrunk away from the bone, and still wonder how it is we have managed to come upon her and that it is solved and over. She has been there six days.

Then, all afternoon, we wait in the ward while the police are fetched who comb the wood for her other shoe, then fetch the body up to the mortuary. The coroner's assistant, a Scots policeman, comes and takes a statement from me as the one who discovered the body. Then we sit in the attendants' room off the old ladies' ward where Aunty has been this last year, odd bits of conversation filtering through.

'Are you my friend, Kitty?' says one of the nurses to an old girl who is braying with her spoon on the tray that fastens her in. 'Nay, Kitty. I thought you were my friend so why are you banging?'

Old ladies make endlessly for the door, only to be

turned back. A woman walks about outside, one hand on her head, the other clasped to her cheek. From time to time nurses come in and talk, one saying how, though it had never happened before, Mr Blackburn, the charge nurse, had said it would happen if they could not lock the doors . . . as they can't under the current Mental Health Act, so half their time is spent fielding these lost and wandering creatures who are trying to reach the outside world or, like Aunty Kathleen, 'just having a meander down'. Mr Blackburn and his wife had searched and searched and now, having lost her, the atmosphere on the ward is terrible.

In the statement I give my profession as Company Director. There will be a post-mortem this evening and an inquest next week. We drive home, where I have a cold bath, then go off ten minutes later down to Airedale, where Mam is sleepy and slow but rational, talking of her life when she gets better. If she gets better, she says, and her eyes fill with tears.

Gordon is still concerned that the police did not begin searching until Thursday, a whole day after she disappeared and even then only looked half-heartedly. I am more philosophical about it, or lazier, Gordon seeing it as a situation which can be corrected if only it is pointed out whereas I see it as a reflection of the value we place on the old and think it useless to raise the matter.

A life varies in social importance. We set most value on the life of a child. Had a child been missing, the whole of the police force plus dozens of volunteers would have been systematically combing the waste ground where we wandered so aimlessly this morning. They would have covered the area in wide sweeps from the hospital and in due course she would have been discovered, perhaps still alive; certainly she would have been found had she been a child, which in many senses she was, except that her life was behind not before her. Had she been a teenager they would probably not have looked, unless there was suspicion of foul play, and maybe if there had been any thought of foul play with Aunty Kathleen that would have fetched the police out too, though no willing volunteers such as turn out to look for someone young. Aunty Kathleen's life was at its lowest point of social valuation. She was seventy-three. She was senile. She was demented, and she was of no class or economic importance. When she was found concern centred not on her fate but on how it reflected on the staff of the hospital and the efficiency of the police force. Even in death she was of marginal importance as a person.

There is, too, under it all, the unspoken recognition that if such pathetic creatures escape – or 'wander off', since escape implies intention and she was long since incapable of that – then the death that they die, of exposure, hypothermia or heart failure, is better than the one they would otherwise have died: sitting vacantly in a chair year after year, fed by hand, soiling themselves, waiting without thought or feeling until the decay of the body catches up with the decay of the mind and they can cross the finishing line together. No, to die at the foot of a wall by the verge of the motorway is a better death than that.

Thursday, 12 September 1974. I drive over slowly to Lancaster Moor on a warm, misty day. So nervous of being late I had booked an alarm call for eight a.m. though the inquest is not until ten-thirty. Hanging over me for more than a week, I have almost come to think of it as a trial. I imagine the row, the hospital reprimanded for carelessness, the police for not conducting a rigorous search and the press wanting to know what I feel about it all.

We sit in a small room in the main building above the bowling green and the dreadful roaring motorway. Stand on the terrace of the hospital and you can see the trees in question. The copse even has a name, it is mentioned in evidence. Stockabank Wood.

Present are Nurse Blackburn, Bill, Aunty Kathleen's husband, and me, plus reporters, who do not seem like reporters at all, one a woman in thick glasses looking like a crafts instructor, the other an insurance agent.

It is not the coroner, but his deputy – and by the looks of him his grandfather, an old man in a bulky overcoat, sharp white stubble, glasses . . . and a manner reminiscent of Miles Malleson. He takes each witness through their statement, with very few questions asked. The pathologist, who looks as if he himself has died from exposure several days before, describes the post-mortem in a bored, blurred monotone . . . the lesions on the skin, the weight of the brain slightly lighter than average, the thickening of the arteries, several gallstones, many gastric ulcers. 'Would these be painful?' 'Not necessarily.'

Heart in good condition; some emphysema. Death due to exposure aggravated by senile dementia.

The coroner records a verdict of misadventure almost before the words are out of the pathologist's mouth. Simpson, the coroner's officer, mutters to the two press about not mentioning my name, there is some hand-shaking and expressions of sympathy and I come away in the misty sunshine relieved and, for the first time in many weeks, happy. I have coffee in Lancaster, shop and drive back home. In the afternoon I blackberry up Crummock and a man passing up the lane says, 'I bet you're often mistaken for a television personality.'

Unrecorded is how all this week Mam has slowly been getting better, talking a little and taking a more measured view of what her life is to be. I arrive at the hospital at seven and she is already sitting in her blue raincoat and hat ready for our walk along the corridor for a cup of tea. On Tuesday I told her about Aunty Kathleen and how she had died in her sleep. She weeps a little . . . just as, coming into the house on Sunday, she wept remembering Dad. But it passes. And at least she weeps.

My anxiety that there should be no fuss and the word I had with the coroner's clerk which led him to take the reporters on one side were less to do with my own situation than with my mother's. In 1974 the tabloids were not so hungry for sensation as they are now, though even today 'Playwright Finds Aunt's Body' wouldn't be much of a circulation booster. What was bothering me was not the *Mirror* or the *Sun* but the local paper, the *Lancaster Guardian*, an old-fashioned weekly publication where inquests were a staple item, a whole page devoted exclusively to the proceedings of the coroner's court. The paper was read in the village, sold in the village shop, and though there was nothing to be ashamed of in my aunty's death or in the manner of her dying, my mother was about to come back home from the hospital and with the stigma of recurrent mental illness try to face life there alone. The last thing I wanted, or she would have wanted, was for it to be known that her sister too had ended up mentally deranged, dying tragically as a result. What kind of family was this, I imagined people saying, where two sisters were mentally unstable. No, the less said about Aunty Kathleen's death the better.

Vague as Mam was about recent events, including even Dad's death, it was not difficult to evade her questions about Kathleen. I told her that she had died in her sleep, and even the few relatives we had left in Leeds were not told the whole story. 'It's funny Kathleen going like that,' Mam would sometimes say. 'Because she was always a strong woman.'

It perhaps will seem strange and even hypocritical that my precautions against the circumstances of Aunty Kathleen's death becoming known did not then recall to me the similar precautions that had covered up the suicide of my grandfather and which I had found so shocking. That it did not was perhaps because I saw it not as my own shame or any reflection of prejudices that I held but as a necessary precaution to protect my mother against the prejudices of others. But perhaps that was how my grandmother had reasoned fifty years before? At any rate, the similarity (and the symmetry) never occurred to me at the time, and even had it done so I would not have acted differently. As it is I am so fearful of the news coming out I do not look in the *Lancaster Guardian* to see if the discovery of the body is reported or if there is a later account of the proceedings at the inquest, and if friends in the village see such reports no one ever mentions it to me.

Aunty Myra's cremation had been at Lytham St Annes; Aunty Kathleen's is at Morecambe, one as featureless as the other. Kathleen's husband then presumably takes himself off to Australia and is, I imagine, long since dead, as are all the Peels, though my mother perhaps because disencumbered of all her memories lives on into her nineties.

My mother never learns the true circumstances of her sister's death. My brother and I do not tell her, and even before her memory begins to slip away she seldom enquires. Whether Kathleen's disappearance and discovery were reported at the time I never know, and it's not until twenty years later when I am beginning to find out more of the circumstances of my grandfather's death that I eventually look in the archives of the *Lancaster Guardian* for what reports there had been.

The *Lancaster Guardian* is an old-fashioned newspaper with a splendidly parochial attitude to what constitutes news. 'Smelly Sow led to Rolling Pin Attack' is one item; 'Man Steals Two Skirts Off Line' another. The paper for 6

September 1974 reports the finding of Aunty Kathleen's body under the heading:

FOUND DEAD

The body of a patient who had been at Lancaster Moor Hospital for the last six months was found in a small wood about a mile from the hospital at 2 p.m. on Tuesday September 3rd. She was Mrs Kathleen Elizabeth Roach (73) formerly of 26 Ruskin Drive, Bare, Morecambe. She was reported missing on Wednesday of last week and police with dogs have been searching since them It is understood that the body was found by people walking in the wood. The coroner has been informed.

I look for the report of the inquest in the following week's paper. It is not even mentioned.

In 1985 I go over to Ypres in Belgium to search for the grave of Uncle Clarence, my mother's brother killed there in 1917.* I am fifty-one, which is about the age most people get interested in their origins, family history one of those

* See 'Uncle Clarence', in *Writing Home*, p. 22

enlivening occupations that these days take up the slack of early retirement. The sense that my own departure is not as distant as it has always seemed adds some mild urgency to the quest, but having found this grave, and having written about it, even then I don't go on to try and find out about the only remaining mystery in my family's history, the death of my grandfather.

However, in 1988 I make a documentary, *Dinner at Noon*, at the Crown Hotel in Harrogate. Without originally intending it to be autobiographical it turns out to be so, with reminiscences of some of the holidays we had had as children and my feelings about our failings as a family. It's perhaps in consequence of this that, stuck in Leeds one afternoon with a couple of hours to wait for a train, I go up to the Registrar's Office and get a copy of my grandfather's death certificate and now, furnished with the exact date of his death, 26 April 1925, I walk along the Headrow to the City Reference Library to see whether I can find out more.

It's a library I have known since I was a boy, when I used to go there in the evenings to do my homework and where I would often see sad old men consulting back numbers of the local papers, done up in a great swatch like a sagging piano accordion. Now it's my turn. However, expecting to be lumbered thus, I'm relieved to find that all the back numbers of newspapers are now on microfilm and so take my place in front of a screen, much as I used to do at a slightly later date but in the same library, on vacations from Oxford when I was reading the Memoranda Rolls of the medieval Exchequer. Now it is the death of my grandfather and I find it in the *Armley and Wortley News*, dated 1 May 1925, the item headed:

NEW WORTLEY MAN DROWNED AT CALVERLEY
Strange Conversation with Friendly Constable

The tragic story of how a policeman, after having been in conversation with a friend who was depressed, noticed the strangeness of the latter's action and followed him only to find that he was dead, was told at an inquest at Calverley on Tuesday on William Peel (55) of 35 Bruce Street, New Wortley, who was found drowned in the canal at Calverley on Sunday.

Mary Ann Peel, wife of the deceased man, said that her husband was formerly a clothing shop manager. In October he became out of work and recently he acquired an empty shop in which to start on his own as a gentleman's outfitter. He had opened this shop last Tuesday and had been somewhat depressed, wondering if he would be a success. On Sunday last he left home just after noon. He did not say where he was going. Police Constable Goodison said that on Sunday last he boarded a Rodley tramcar in company with Peel. He inquired how the new shop in Wellington Road was getting along. Peel seemed rather depressed about it. When Goodison was leaving the tram at Cockshott Lane, Peel's parting words were, 'Goodbye old chap. I hope you make better headway than I have done.'

Constable Goodison left the car and was walking towards his home when, after thinking about what had been said, decided to go back and follow Peel.

'I caught the first available tram to Rodley terminus,' said Goodison. 'I made inquiries there, but failed to find any trace of him. I then searched along the canal bank in the direction of Calverley and when near the University boathouse I saw what appeared to be a stump in the water.'

He judged it to be the body of a man and went to obtain a boat hook. At 3.30 along with two other constables he recovered the body, which he at once identified as that of Mr Peel.

Mr Peel's hat, coat and stick were found on the canal bank, and three letters addressed to his wife, friends and relations were found in the coat pocket. In one of the letters was the passage 'I am going to Rodley by tram this afternoon, and my intention is to find a watery grave in the canal between Rodley and Apperley Bridge.'

A verdict that the deceased man drowned himself while suffering from depression was recorded.

(Interred New Wortley Cemetery.)

Some of the saddest circumstances were not reported at the inquest. When her father had gone out on his last errand Mam was not in the house as she and Dad had gone on a tram-ride themselves, out into the country, courting, but before he left the house that Sunday morning her father had kissed his wife and tried to kiss the other two daughters, but Kathleen would have none of it and as he was going out she said, 'Yes, go out . . . and come back a man,' words that she must have recalled without ever being able to call them back when later that day she had to identify him. But I hear in those words, too, harsh and melodramatic as they are, an echo of that same pent-up rage and frustration that my mother's depression came to induce in me.

Though I now know the precise location of the drowning, near the university boathouse, it's another year at least before I take myself along to look at the place – these involuntary intermissions such a feature of the unravelling of this mystery they call for an explanation. Hardly due to pressure of work or any conscious disinclination, these delays, I see now, are to do with appeasing the dead (the dead being my father as well as my grandfather) and shame at indulging a curiosity I still find unseemly.

My father would not have approved of it nor, I'm pretty sure, would my grandmother. As for my mother, she is by this time no longer in a state of mind where approval or disapproval means very much. How can she disapprove of a son whom she seldom recognises or have feelings about the death of a father she no longer recalls?

Still, while there is no doubt in my own mind that I will go and look at the place, and in due course write it up, these misgivings are enough to reinforce my reluctance. So that knowing I need to locate the spot on the canal that is near the university boathouse, when I find on the OS map for Rodley that there is no trace of a boathouse I am almost relieved, and put it off for another year. I have actually never heard of the university having a boat club, and whether it has one now I doubt. But in 1925 Leeds University is still young, the boat club perhaps a bid to hike what had hitherto been just the Yorkshire College up the scale a bit, rowing, after all, what proper university students do. So eventually I do the sensible thing and look up an older map, and finding that there is (or was) a boathouse after all, with no more excuse drive down to Leeds to find it.

The canal in question is the Leeds–Liverpool and running

parallel with it across the valley is the railway, which in 1925 would have been the LMS going up to Keighley and Skipton. In between the canal and the railway is the river, the Aire. Though neither river nor dale has the same picturesque associations as the Wharfe, say, or the Nidd, the Aire is Charles Kingsley's river, the river in *The Water Babies*. Flowing clear out of Malham Cove, it is scarcely at Skipton ten miles away before it slows and thickens and starts to sidle its way through mud banks and the factories and tanneries of Keighley. Unswum and unfished, by the time it reaches Leeds it is as much a drain as it is a river, and at Kirkstall when I was a child it would sometimes steam as it slid through spears of blackened willow-herb past the soot-stained ruins of the abbey. It's hard to imagine that this spot had once been as idyllic and lost to the world as Fountains or Rievaulx, or fancy the monks fetching their sheep down this same valley from Skipton and Malham, where the lands of Kirkstall adjoin those of Fountains.

Rodley is beyond Kirkstall and on the way to Bingley. That trams came this far out of Leeds seems astonishing now, particularly as there is a long hill running down into Rodley, the haul up which must have been at the limit of the trams' capabilities. Down this hill in his Sunday suit and hat came my grandfather.

At Rodley today there is a marina of sorts and the lock has been done up and artful setts laid as part of some environmental scheme. A heritage trail begins or ends here and there are flower beds and whitened stones, much as there used to be outside the guardroom at Pontefract, where I started National Service, and that's what this looks like a bit, and prompts the reflection that some of what passes for care for the environment is just bulling-up, picking up the litter, weeding the cobbles, painting the kerbs . . . a prissy sort of neatness that panders to a sergeant major's feminine notion of what looks nice.

I walk along the canal away from the lock. There is a pub, haunt of the narrow-boat fraternity, I imagine, or a nice little run-out from Leeds; a rusty dredger; a small gasometer, not these days the blot on the landscape it must once have been, preserved and painted now as part of the environmental scheme. A retired couple march past in matching anoraks, walking a Labrador.

Here is a broad-planked swing bridge, for cattle to cross presumably. No boathouse, though, and I walk on, surprised at how far I have come from the lock and wondering at the persistence of Constable Goodison that Sunday afternoon, who didn't know but only suspected and who might, as he must have kept telling himself, running down the towpath and scanning the water, just have been imagining things. People often sound depressed, after all; he'd probably walked it off.

A train scuds past en route for Morecambe and another heading for Leeds: 'Shipley-joining tickets?' the conductor will be saying. Just here the canal, the railway, the river and the road all run parallel, and just over the hill to the north is Leeds and Bradford Airport. It's like one of those fanciful landscapes in the boys' books of childhood in which one setting is made to comprehend transport in all its forms: a car, a train, a boat, a plane all going their separate ways as a man (giving the human scale) walks by the canal.

Across the valley is the factory of Sandoz Chemicals, which laces the spring breeze with the scent of lavatories; but look the other way and it is all fields still, the tower of Calverley Church on the horizon and the woods dropping steeply to the canal. And now there is a raised mound, set back from the bank where there are some stones and a tangle of silver birch and sycamore. I trample about in the undergrowth and see that there are foundations here and that this must be the place, only what was once a boathouse is now just a copse, a sinister word nowadays, a setting for sexual assault, the site of shallow graves: a copse is where bodies are found. Aunty Kathleen was in a copse.

On the other side of it and below the canal is the river, a better place to drown oneself perhaps as it's away from the path and with none to see. But there is a bank to be negotiated, mud to be waded through and the water like sludge. The canal is more wholesome; an element of fastidiousness discernible even in self-destruction. Besides, the bank is steep and the water deep, and it's likely Grandad Peel knew where he was coming. Fond of what was then called nature study, he must have taken the same tram-ride and walked this way before, past the boathouse and the water deep enough at the edge to take the boats. These days there would have been rowing on a Sunday but not then, nor many people about either, not straight after Sunday dinner. I imagine men in Sunday suits, dinner interrupted, running along the bank with boathooks. This, I think, is how one would begin it in a film: men in dark suits, running. But why should they run? He was past running for, given up as soon as he had stepped into the water, this man who could be mistaken for a tree stump.

I stand looking at the black water and I wonder whether Grandma ever came to look. Probably not, which makes it worse that I am here, tracking down the place where someone I never knew and about whom I know nothing did away with himself, long before I was born. Have I nothing better to do? Or rather, have I nothing better to write about? I think of the notes he left, the neatly folded coat, the hat and stick . . . the little pile that marked his grave.

Somebody is coming, a woman briskly walking her dog on a leash, and seeing her I am aware how odd and possibly threatening I must look, a middle-aged man standing staring into the water – and suddenly I am my grandfather. I turn and walk back, the dog straining towards me and growling as I pass.

❧

'Dad. Dad.'

Mam calls down from her bedroom wanting me to go up and like a child she has to be sure she has my attention before she will deliver her message. Except that I cannot answer her, cannot even say 'Yes?' without confirming her assumption that I am my father. It's a delusion that comes in patches, so that when it passes she is left with a sense of ancient horror.

'We haven't done anything wrong, have we? Neither of us has done anything wrong?'

And the fear that something has happened 'between us' becomes another version of the shameful secret that the car waiting in the car park is on watch for, that the television is tuned to detect and the man hiding in the wardrobe ready to jump out and punish.

Saigon is much in the news and her delusions now begin to include helicopters and ladders at the window. She calls upstairs one morning to say that there is a pigeon outside with a message. At the third time of asking I abandon my attempt to work and wearily go down, telling her that she's imagining things. But there is a pigeon on the doorstep, a racer I suppose that has flown off course, and it does carry a message though it's only the name of the owner. On another occasion she struggles to convince me that there are three huge birds in the garden. I ridicule this but finally go into the garden with ill grace, and of course there they are: three peacocks from the Hall.

Liberal analysts, and in particular the followers of R. D. Laing, if there are still any such, would seize on these misunderstandings as demonstrating how families conspire to label one of their number deluded even when he or she is speaking the truth. Right about the racing pigeon and the peacocks, is she right, too, in thinking I want her out of the way?

Because that's how the descent into delusion always ends up, with Mam going yet again to hospital.

'I think we're on the hospital trail again,' says the cleaning woman in *Soldiering On*: that was always how Dad used to put it and now I do the same.

'You'll kill me if you go on in this way,' I say melodramatically, Mam having woken me up three times in the night. I am thinking of my father, and it takes some self-restraint not to say 'You'll kill me too', though that is what I mean. Of course the only way she is killing me is, in the way of women with men, not letting me have my own way, nor allowing me to lead the relatively liberated life I've lately discovered in London. No chance of any of that at home.

There are periods, though, almost of normality when we get along well enough and yet even then I can see, unreason apart, why it is she so easily conflates my father and myself, if only because I slip so naturally into what had been his retired routine: doing the shopping, much of the cooking and cleaning, and every afternoon taking her for a little run in the car.

One theory advanced, a little too readily I thought, by various of Mam's therapists over the years was that she had slipped into depression because when Dad retired she was deprived of her function in the household. This was to some extent true, as after Dad gave up work he did the baking and most of the cooking and cleaning so there was very little in the house for Mam to do. Her depressions, so the theory went, were called up to provide a reason for the sudden pointlessness of her life.

This has always seemed to me a little glib as Dad had always helped in the house all their married life. They shared the housework as they shared everything else. Retirement may have accentuated this, but the pattern was as it had always been.

On the draining board in the kitchen – which they still

called the scullery – there would often be a pan of potatoes, peeled and ready for boiling, and a pan of sprouts and carrots likewise. Dad would have done them first thing that morning – or even the night before; with not enough to occupy his time jobs like this would get done earlier and earlier and long before they needed to be, one meal no sooner cleared than the next prepared.

I have seen similar premature preparations in the homes of other retired couples and it speaks of lives emptied of occupation and proper activity, so that squalor and slatternliness seem almost cheerful by comparison.

Two such pans would be a revealing shot in a documentary film. The two pans in the kitchen, the two people by the fire. Or one. Had he been alone, had Mam 'gone first', that would still have been Dad's way, though he was not without interests, reading, gardening, playing his violin. But excepting always when he had his hands full with my mother there was always time to spare. Had he been fonder of male company or she of company of any sort things might have been different. But they were, as they had always been, inseparable, 'your Dad and me', 'your Mam and me' always the phrases most often on their lips. Joining the Women's Institute when she came to the village, Mam would go off on their trips, but Dad would as often as not go too, utterly unembarrassed that he was the only man in the party.

As her depressions became more frequent such outings must have seemed almost unimaginable, the only outings Dad was now required to make his daily trek to the hospital.

Still, Mam's hankerings for society were not quite extinguished and after his death, in periods of remission, the social yearnings to which she had always been prone would tend to return. They were faltering a little by this time and the cocktail party, a long-standing ambition, was now firmly off the agenda. But television gave her aspirations a fresh direction as, tapping into a new potential audience, it began to preach the delights of retirement and the rolling back of the frontiers of old age through a more active use of leisure.

Trying to wean her off my company and making one of my many attempts to get her to stand on her own feet, I'd been to London for a couple of days, the first time she'd been alone in the house since my father died. When I came back I was encouraged when she said, 'I've started going to classes.'

'What in?'

'Pottery.'

'That's good. Didn't you once go to painting classes?'

'Did I? Oh yes. Only then he said it was for beginners whereas when I got there I found most of them could do it right well, they weren't beginners at all. I think that's what it is with classes, people just go to show off what they can do.'

'Well, it'll be a way of rubbing shoulders.'

And so for a while she went. 'Clay Night' she used to call it, and would come back as often as not with a Stone Age-type ashtray she had made . . . not that anybody in the house smoked.

At such times normality seemed within reach. I even thought she might learn to drive, and gave her one disastrous lesson. I smile to think of it now, but why is it still so inconceivable, I ask myself. I certainly asked myself then, and I'm sure lectured her on the subject, how other people's mothers learned to drive, went Old Tyme Dancing, did aerobics: a friend of mine's mother, not much younger than Mam, was Lord Mayor of Blackburn; what was it about our family that we were disqualified from normal social life, and which kept Dad out of the pub, Mam out of the WI and me, I suppose, out of the Garrick? Clay Night or no Clay

Night, it isn't long before we are back sitting on the chair in the passage, lurking about the landing and never stirring out except to scuttle between the door and the car.

'There are lights on in the wood. I think there are people there.'

'It's the Children's Home.'

'No, besides that.'

'What do you want, Mam?'

'To be hung. You won't send me away, will you?'

'No.'

But as Laing and Co. might smugly note, 'No' meant 'Yes' and in due course she was back in hospital.

I knew the doctor in charge as we had been at school together in Leeds. Slightly older than me, he had played Canon Chasuble in *The Importance of Being Earnest* and I had played Cecily. Like me he had been very religious, and I wondered if he was as uneasy about his childhood self as I was about mine. Fortunately the subject didn't come up. I was always nervous of discussing anything but the matter in hand with my mother's various psychotherapists for fear they were taking notes on me too, and that whatever I said, however lightly, would be taken down and held in evidence against me; I was part of the equation.

And perhaps I was, and perhaps Dad was too; maybe we had both helped to make her into this helpless, cringing creature, though how I would find hard to say. She has made me timid too, I thought, hedging round our childhoods with all sorts of TB-fuelled fears and prohibitions that hung about well into middle age. But that is a long road to go down; she is seventy; better to patch her up (more tablets) and sit it out.

And in due course she begins to come round again, though whether this is thanks to the medication or the normal time span to these things I never know. Occasionally she will talk of Kathleen's death, wondering how she could go 'just like that. She was always such a bouncer. What was it exactly?'

'Her heart,' I would say, 'or else pneumonia.' But never, of course, the facts, so that now my secret matches hers, though that is not quite a secret any more and she will from time to time talk about her father and in particular of the Sunday when he died. But the reticence of forty years is hard to throw off, and she does not respond to questions and still feels that it is not a proper subject for conversation.

There are many opportunities for that now as I live at home in the village. It is only for six or eight months, though to me it seems much longer. I am trying to write a play about some contemporaries who every summer rent a villa abroad – the sort of holiday I used to go on myself before being saddled with my mother. Someone is killed in an air crash, who is, I suppose, my friend Francis Hope, who died in the Paris air crash in 1974. It isn't going well, so I don't suppose that with my depression about the play I am any easier to live with than Mam and her depression about practically everything else. I finish the play and it's turned down, a year's work, as I see it, wasted.

My brother and his wife, who are always more decent with my mother than I am, eventually shoulder the burden and Mam moves down to Bristol to live with them. There she stays, regularly hospitalised for depression, with even the periods in between tentative and precarious, never an unshadowed return to the cheerful, funny, affectionate woman she once had been.

Company seems to suit her, or so another hospital psychotherapist suggests, and so she graduates easily from one sort of institution to another, moving directly from the mental hospital to a series of old people's homes in Weston-super-Mare. In the home her memory begins to fail, and as it does so her depression lifts, leaving in its wake a vapid and generalised benevolence.

'This is my friend,' she says of any of the residents who happen to be in the room, and as often as not plants a kiss on the slightly startled cheek.

Going for a run in the car she is full of wonderment at the world, transformed as it is by her promiscuous magnanimity. 'What a lovely council estate,' she says of some grim new development. 'What charming houses.'

Except that now her language is beginning to go, and planted in front of a vast view over Somerset she laughs and says, 'Oh, what a lovely . . . lot of about.'

With my mother losing her memory I find myself wondering whether it can be put down to the ECT she has been given in the past, and so, therefore, if we are to some extent to blame. The stock answer to such questioning is that the memory loss associated with ECT is in the short term, particularly that period of confusion which follows immediately after the treatment, and that otherwise it has no measurable effect on the memory proper.

I am not wholly convinced of this, if only because the proponents of ECT must nowadays feel themselves so blamed and beleaguered that they are forced into demanding from its opponents evidence of its ill effects that is hard and fast and, in the nature of things, impossible to provide. What causes loss of memory? Nobody can be certain. It might be ECT in Mam's case, though her mother had begun to lose her memory at about the same age and would, no doubt, have lost it just as completely as her daughter had she not died in the interim. So both mother and daughter lost their memory; one had ECT, the other not.

Even had we been told that ECT would lead ultimately to a failure of memory in the long term I am not sure, given the circumstances, that we would have done anything differently. Unreachable in her despair Mam was unliveable with, her condition inspiring such strain in Dad that his health was as much a factor as hers.

In the end it was her disease that killed him long before it killed her, the strain of daily visiting over weeks and months and the fifty-mile drive they involved fetching on a heart attack. So, though licensing ECT may have been the wrong thing to do, I feel no remorse, and still think, as I did in that cinema in Oxford Street, when the controversy periodically surfaces that the opponents of ECT don't really know the half of it.

There are comic moments. After one visit I tell Miss Shepherd that Mam's memory is failing her and that I am not sure she knows who I am.

'Well, it's not surprising she doesn't remember you,' said Gloucester Crescent's resident moralist, 'she doesn't see you very often.'

A more common attempt at consolation was to say that, though her memory for the recent past might be failing, it would be compensated for by a more detailed recall of the remoter past. This proves not to be the case. As Mam slowly forgets my father so she forgets her mother and her two sisters, and even eventually who she is herself; the present goes and the past with it.

'Do you remember Dad?' I ask her.

'Oh yes. I remember your Dad.'

'What was he like?'

'Your Dad? Oh well,' and she studies a bit, 'well, he was a love.'

'And do you know who I am?'

Mam and Dad with Julie, their first grandchild

'You're a love too,' and she laughs.

'But who am I?'

'Well, now then . . . you're my son, aren't you?'

'Yes. And what's my name?'

'Oh, I don't know *that*,' and she laughs again, as if this isn't a piece of information she could be reasonably expected to have, and moreover isn't in the least distressed not to have. She isn't seemingly distressed by anything much nowadays, even by the hip she broke sometime in 1986 and which has never healed properly. It's painful when she moves and I see her wince, but her memory span is so short it mitigates the discomfort and I'm not sure if without memory there can be such a thing as continuous pain. Sitting with her in the large hot bedroom overlooking the bay at Weston-super-Mare, I occupy myself with such vaguely philosophical speculations, watching as she smoothes the sheet with her thin, blue-veined hands, smoothing and stretching, stretching and smoothing all the weary afternoon.

She has long since ceased to wear her own clothes, which probably wouldn't fit her anyway since she's now so much thinner. These days she's kitted out from a pool of frocks and cardigans that the home must have accumulated and put into anything that's more or less her size.

To begin with we, or rather my brother, protest about this and insist that one of her original frocks be found, so long as it isn't actually adorning one of the other old ladies, which as often as not it is. In which case it's promised for 'next time' or 'when we change her'. Still, as Gordon argues, in a world where so much must seem strange, to be wearing a familiar frock may be a comfort.

As time goes on, though, this argument carries less weight. When she can't recognise her own children and doesn't even know what children are, how can she recall 'the little coatee I got at Richard Shops' all those years ago? Sometimes I'm not sure she's in her own glasses, and maybe her teeth would be a problem if they ever put them in; but then her mouth may have shrunk anyway, so perhaps like her clothes they don't fit either.

So when I go in I'm no longer surprised to find her sitting there in a fluorescent-orange cardigan she would in happier days have unhesitatingly labelled 'common'; or that the skirt she has hitched well above her scrawny knees is Tricel or Crimplene or some tufted material she wouldn't have been seen dead in.

And it isn't only the cardigan and the frock that aren't hers. She has even acquired someone else's name. The nurses, who are not really nurses but just jolly girls who don't mind this kind of job, aren't over-particular about names and call her Lily.

'Hello, Lily, how are we today? Let's lift you up, Lily. You're falling right over.'

'Her name's Lilian,' I venture.

'I know,' says the ministering angel, propping her back up, 'only we call her Lily, don't we, Lily? Give us a kiss.' And vacantly Mam smiles and gives her a kiss.

'You know what a kiss is, don't you, Lily?'

And she does, just, but it will be the next thing to go.

'She's with my brother,' I say if anyone asks who knew her in the village. 'It's down in Bristol.'

To admit she's in a home in Weston-super-Mare is itself a confession of failure, with the nowhereness of Weston a part of it, an acknowledgement that we have run out of patience, washed our hands of her and put her away in Weston, as it might be Reykjavik or Archangel, it seems so remote.

And if I do specify the location I'll often add, 'Except she's not there, you know. She's not anywhere,' and I explain that all her faculties have gone. It's then that people nod understandingly and say 'Alzheimer's'.

'Well,' I say, 'she's failing.' Or has failed, as she now can scarcely speak. But whether it's Alzheimer's I don't know,

as she's never had a brain scan that would prove the point
. . . though why is the point worth proving except for statistical purposes? But since for twenty-five years or so she's been in and out of institutions – hospitals, mental hospitals and homes – it wouldn't surprise me if her blankness now is partly the result and that she has become institutionalised. This would explain the decay of her powers of speech and her inability to walk just as plausibly as any specific disease.

But my vagueness (about her vagueness) has another, less creditable side. I'm reluctant to ascribe her situation to Alzheimer's because, without it being exactly modish or fashionable, it is a disease or a condition that gets a good deal of coverage as one of the scourges of our time. People are frightened of it; they make jokes about it; it's mainstream stuff. I don't mean that I'd prefer her to be suffering from, living with, dying from something a bit more *exclusive*, it's just that I wouldn't want anyone to think that by putting her situation down to Alzheimer's I was in any way jumping on a bandwagon.

A diagnosis, which is, essentially, a naming, puts someone in a category. Neither Mam nor Dad was ever a big joiner, 'not being able to mix' both their affliction and their boast. So now, faced with a choice of enrolling her in the ranks of those diagnosed and named as having Alzheimer's, I still prefer to keep my mother separate, so that she can die as she has lived, keeping herself to herself.

～

Except, of course, she does not die. Her bed is in a high bay-windowed room on the first floor, the house one of a row of granite mansions strung like battlements along the side of the hill that overlooks the bay. The prospect from the window is vast, taking in the town, the sands and the distant sea, and some hills beyond that I take to be Wales. The room, though, ignores the view, the plastic-covered chairs arranged in a row with their backs to the window so as to catch all of the place's diminishing life.

Here live four women, each with a high cream-painted hospital bed, a chair, a washbasin and a locker. All the women are incontinent and all are catheterised, a bottle of faint piss tilted under each chair. Cloyingly warm, the room has no particular smell (no smell of urine I suppose I mean), the air refreshed by frequent blasts of Woodland Glade or Ocean Breeze. That if anyone chose to open a window there could be a proper ocean breeze goes by the way.

On the top of the lockers are family snaps: the lurid single photographs of children, or rather grandchildren, of the sort that are routinely taken at primary school; photos of family outings, dead husbands, dead sons. 'Happier days'. There are birthday cards kept long after the big day: 'To the Best Mum in the World', 'To Nan from Toni, Michelle and little Christopher'.

With its broad landings and cavernous rooms, it's hard to think that this gaunt pile in Weston-super-Mare can ever have been a private house or imagine the family that lived in it. Everywhere is carpeted with the predominant colours orange and brown, and with the staircase wide enough to accommodate a chair lift.

'I've been on that thing,' Mam said in her early days here, then adding contemptuously, 'it's nowt.' It was as if it were the Big Dipper.

None of the residents are black yet, though there are one or two black nurses and several cleaners. When in due course blacks take their place among the patients here and in similar establishments it will, I suppose, signal a sort of victory, though hardly one to be rejoiced over as the price of it is a common enslavement to age and infirmity.

The residents are almost entirely women, the only man a voice from a distant room where he is presumably bedfast. I see a handyman occasionally, standing on a ladder changing light bulbs or dismantling a bed. He seldom speaks. There is the clash of a kitchen somewhere in the back, two trolleys outside a door, waiting.

The staff are young mainly and seldom stay long, the only attendant I recognise from the ten years or so I have been coming here now old herself. Doing less and less and with her help increasingly superfluous, she has gradually declined until now she is more nursed than nursing. Shedding her overall and wrapover pinny, she has taken her place among the rest, sitting in the bay window dozing and not looking at the view.

The shallow waves lap over the sands and at night ropes of lights prick out the promenade.

I sit by my mother's bed. She does not look at me or look at all, her eyes open but her gaze dull and unattached. I note her wild eyebrows, the coated tongue, the long lobes of her ears and the downy, crimped and slightly stained skin of her upper lip. A dispassionate inventory this, taken holding her slack hand, which I occasionally bend down and kiss.

She speaks infrequently, and when she does speak it makes less sense, with her words gradually becoming a babble. Second childhood in my mother's case is not just a phrase but a proper description of how skills learned in the first years of her life are gradually unlearned at its end and in reverse order: speech has come out of babble and now reverts to it.

A family drives onto the beach, lets out a romping dog, then arranges the canvas chairs. A man and a child set off barefooted across the sands to the distant sea, as on the promenade an ice-cream van sounds its glutinous unfinished song.

I have talked to only one of the women here besides Mam . . . Hilda, who in the days when she could talk told me she came from Darwen. Now, not knowing where she is, did she realise she had ended up in this unentrancing corner of Somerset she would be as puzzled as my mother whose own odyssey began in Leeds.

The turnover of residents is quite rapid since whoever is quartered in this room is generally in the later stages of dementia. But that is not what they die of. None of these lost women can feed herself and to feed them properly, to spoon in sufficient mince and mashed carrot topped off with rhubarb and custard to keep them going, demands the personal attention of a helper, in effect one helper per person. Lacking such one-to-one care, these helpless creatures slowly and quite respectably starve to death.

This is not something anybody acknowledges, not the matron or the relatives (if, as is rare, they visit), and not the doctor who makes out the death certificates. But it is so.

And if Mam has survived as long as she has it is because, though she can no longer feed herself, she nevertheless is anxious to eat; her appetite remains good and so she is easy (and satisfying) to feed. I spoon in the mince and carrot, catching the bits that dribble down her chin and letting her lick the spoon.

'Joined the clean plate club, Lily,' says the girl who is feeding Hilda, her neighbour. 'Aren't you a good girl?'

Hilda, grim, small-eyed and with a little curved nose and a face like a finch, is not a good girl, turning her head when the spoon approaches, keeping her teeth clamped shut with the spoon tapping to get in.

'Knock, knock,' says the girl.

Somewhere a phone rings. So, leaving the mince, the girl goes to answer it and does not come back. Ten minutes later comes a different girl who clears away the cold mince and carrot and substitutes rhubarb crumble.

While Mam polishes off hers, Hilda remains obdurate, beak closed.

'Don't want your sweet, Hilda?'

Hilda doesn't and it is left congealing on the tray while tea in lidded plastic beakers is taken round, which goes untouched also. So another mealtime passes and Hilda is quite caringly and with no malice or cruelty at all pushed one step nearer the grave.

Whose fault is it?

Her own, a little. Her relatives, if she has relatives. And the staff's, of course. But whereas a newspaper might make a horror story out of it, I can't.

Demented or not, if Hilda were a child there would be a story to tell and blame attaching. But Hilda is at the end of her life not the beginning. Even so, were she a Nobel Prize winner, or not a widow from Darwen but the last survivor of Bloomsbury, yes, then an effort might be made. As it is she is gradually slipping away, which is what this place is for.

The water creeps over the sands.

Coming back to London on the train, I am relieved that I have done my perfunctory duty and need not come again for a fortnight or three weeks; I am still uneasy, though, and would be however often I were to visit.

That there is something not right around homes for the elderly is evident in the language associated with them: it's swampy, terms do not quite fit and categories start to slip. A home is not a home but neither is it a hospital nor yet a hotel. What do we call the old people who live (and die) there? Are they residents? Patients? Inmates? No word altogether suits. And who looks after them? Nurses? Not really since very few of them are qualified. As Mam herself pointed out early in her residency:

'They're not nurses, these. Most of them are just lasses.'

And not knowing what to call them makes getting hold of one difficult, not least for the residents. In a hospital it would be 'Nurse!' Here it tends to be 'Hello? Hello?', which said to nobody in particular and sometimes to an empty room already sounds deranged. Of course, calling them by name could be the answer, but though the staff all wear their name tags, names are what these lost women are not good at, not being good at names one of the things that has brought them here in the first place. And what do I call them, a visitor? Even if I cared for the word caring, 'Carer!' is not a word you can call down a corridor.

As it is, and feeling like one of those old-fashioned gentlemen who call every policeman 'Officer', I settle for 'Nurse', remembering at the same time Mrs Catchpole, Alan Bates's mother-in-law, who, incarcerated in the geriatric ward at the Royal Free, remarked bitterly of one such whom she called 'Bouncing Betty': 'She's not as highly qualified as she makes out. And she has very hard hands.'

These blurred classifications – a home that is not a home, a nurse who is not a nurse – arise because strictly speaking the people in homes are not ill; it is not sickness that has brought them here so much as incurable incompetence. They are not dying; they are just incapable of living, though capable of being long-lived nevertheless. My mother lives like this for fifteen years.

Now it is a year later or maybe two years. Nothing has changed except that there are new faces in the three other beds, all of them registering differing degrees of vacancy. None of them can talk, though one of them can shout.

I sit in the upstairs rooms and hold my mother's hand, the skin now just a translucent sheath for the bones, and a hand anyone who comes into the room is free to take and hold as Mam will not mind or even notice. And though there will be no replies forthcoming, having been told it is therapeutic I embark on a conversation.

'Gordon will have been, I expect.

'Set up with their new baby. Grandparents now. You're a great-grandmother. Takes after Ian, Rita says. Fair.

'They're going in for a new fridge apparently. One of those jumbo jobs.'

I have written conversations like this to point up the diminutive stature of our concerns and their persistence even into the jaws of death. But this conversation I now have to fabricate for real is as desultory and depressing as any of my fictions.

'They tell you to talk,' I had once written of a visitor talking to someone unconscious.

'I think it's got past that stage,' says the nurse.

* * *

And so it seems with Mam, as nothing I ever say provokes a response: no smile; no turn of the head even.

The staff do it differently; make a good deal more noise than I do for a start, and one of the maids now erupts into the room and seizes Mam's hand, stroking her face and kissing her lavishly.

'Isn't she a love!

'Aren't you a love!

'Aren't we pretty this morning!

'Who's going to give me a kiss?'

The dialogue makes me wince and the delivery of it seems so much bad acting better directed at a parrot or a Pekinese. But, irritatingly, Mam seems to enjoy it, this grotesque performance eliciting far more of a response than is achieved by my less condescending and altogether more tasteful contribution.

Mam's face twitches into a parody of a smile, her mouth opens in what she must think is a laugh and she waves her hand feebly in appreciation, all going to show, in my view, that taste and discrimination have gone along with everything else.

But then taste has always been my handicap, and so here

when in this sponged and squeegeed bedroom with an audience of indifferent old women I do not care to unbend, call my mother 'chick', fetch my face close to hers and tell her or shout at her how much I love her and how we all love her and what a treasure she is.

Instead, smiling sadly, I lightly stroke her limp hand, so ungarish my display of affection I might be the curate, not the son.

The nurses (or whatever) have more sense. They know they are in a 'Carry On' film. I am playing it like it's *Brief Encounter*.

'Aren't you good, Lily? You've eaten all your mince.'

And Mam purses her lips over her toothless gums for a rewarding kiss. Twenty years ago she would have been as embarrassed by this affectation of affection as I am. But that person is dead, or forgotten anyway, living only in the memory of this morose middle-aged man who turns up every fortnight, if she's lucky, and sits there expecting his affection to be deduced from the way he occasionally takes her hand, stroking the almost transparent skin before putting it sensitively to his lips.

No. Now she is Lily who has eaten all her mince and polished off her Arctic Roll, and her eyes close, her mouth opens and her head falls sideways on the pillow.

'She's a real card is Lily. We always have a laugh.'

'Her name's actually Lilian,' I say primly.

'I know, but we call her Lily.'

The strip lights go on this winter afternoon and I get ready to leave.

I never come away but I think that this may be the last time I shall see her, and it's almost a superstition therefore that before I leave I should make eye contact with her. It's sometimes for the first time as she can spend the whole hour not looking at me or not seeing me if she does. Kissing does not make her see me nor stroking her hand. A loud shout may do so, though, and certainly if I were to squeeze her arm or cause her pain she would look at me then or even cry out. Otherwise, there is this settled indifference to my presence.

To make her see me is not easy. Sometimes it means bringing my head down, my cheek on the coverlet in order to intercept her eye line and obtrude on her gaze. In this absurd position, my head virtually in her lap, I say, 'Goodbye, Mam, goodbye,' trying as I say it (my head pressing into the candlewick) to picture her with Dad and print her face on my memory, Mam laughing on the sands at Filey with Gordon and me, Mam walking on the prom at Morecambe with Grandma. If this produces no satisfactory epiphany (a widening of the eyes, say, or a bit of a smile) I do it again, the spectacle of this middle-aged man knelt down with his head flat on the bed of no more interest to the other old women than it is to my mother.

Getting no response, I kiss her and go to the door, looking back for what I always think will be the last time. What I want to see is her gazing lovingly after me, her eyes brimming with tears or even just looking. But she has not noticed I've gone, and I might never have been in the room at all. I walk to the station.

'You have given the best,' says a hoarding advertising another home, 'now receive the best.' And in a film faintly would come the sound of the geriatric Horst Wessel, that sad and mendacious anthem, 'I am H-A-P-P-Y.'

Once her speech has unravelled, any further deterioration in her personality becomes hard for an onlooker to gauge (and we are all onlookers). Speechless and seemingly beyond reach, she dozes in the first-floor bedroom in the house above the bay, regularly fed and watered, her hair done every fortnight, oblivious of place and time and touch. In the other beds women come and go, or come and die, my mother outlasting them all. On the horizon ships pass and it is as if her own vessel, having sailed, now lies becalmed, anchored on its own horizon, life suspended, death waiting and in the meantime nothing: life holds her in its slack jaw and seems to doze.

So much of my childhood and youth was lived in dread of her death, never seeing that what would unsettle and unstitch my life much more would be the death of my father. It was his going that had cast the burden of care on my brother's family and myself and sent my mother stumbling into her long twilight.

In the event her death is as tranquil and unremarked as one of those shallow ripples licking over the sands that I had watched so many times from her window. All her life she has hoped to pass unnoticed and now she does.

As a boy I could not bear to contemplate her death. Now when it happens I almost shrug. She dies in 1995, I think. That I am not certain of the date and even the year and have to walk down to the graveyard to look at her gravestone to make sure is testimony to how long she has been waiting on the outskirts of mortality. My father's death on 3 August 1974 I never forget. There was before and after. With my mother nothing changes. Did she look at me the last time I took my leave? I can't remember.

Mindful of the snarl on my father's dead face I make no attempt to see my mother dead. Times are different anyway and in the self loving nineties death is enjoying less of a vogue. Besides, there is little point in seeking out reminders of mortality. I am sixty myself now and my own reminder.

So while she rests at the undertaker's my brother and I consult our diaries and decide on a mutually acceptable date for the funeral, and I take the train to Weston-super-Mare for what I hope will be the last time now, though getting off at Nailsea, which is handier for the crematorium. It's a low-key affair, the congregation scarcely bigger than the only other public occasion in my mother's life, the wedding she had shrunk from more than sixty years before.

Of the four or five funerals in this book, only my father's is held in a proper church; the rest, though scattered across England, might all have been in the same place, so uniform is the setting of the municipal crematorium.

The building will be long and low, put up in the sixties, probably, when death begins to go secular. Set in country that is not quite country it looks like the reception area of a tasteful factory or the departure lounge of a small provincial airport confined to domestic flights. The style is contemporary but not eye-catchingly so; this is decorum-led architecture which does not draw attention even to its own merits. The long windows have a stylistic hint of tracery, denomination here a matter of hints, the plain statement of any sort of conviction very much to be avoided.

Related settings might be the waiting area of a motor showroom, the foyer of a small private hospital or a section of a department store selling modern furniture of inoffensive design: dead places. This is the architecture of reluctance, the furnishings of the functionally ill at ease, decor for a place you do not want to be.

It is neat with the neatness ill-omened; clutter means hope and there is none here, no children's drawings, no silly notices. There are flowers, yes, but never a Christmas tree and nothing that seems untidy. The whole function of the place, after all, is to do with tidying something away.

In the long low table a shallow well holds pot plants,

{ 233 }

African violets predominating, tended weekly by a firm that numbers among its clients a design consultancy, an Aids hospice, the boardroom of the local football club and a museum of industrial archaeology.

In the unechoing interior of the chapel soft music plays and grief too is muted, kept modest by the blond wood and oatmeal walls, the setting soft enough to make something so raw as grief seem out of place. It's harder to weep when there's a fitted carpet; at the altar (or furnace) end more blond wood, a table flanked by fins of some tawny-coloured hardwood set in a curved wall covered in blueish-greenish material, softly lit from below. No one lingers in these wings or makes an entrance through them, the priest presiding from a lectern or reading desk on the front of which is a (detachable) cross. A little more spectacular and it could be the setting for a TV game show. Above it all is a chandelier with many sprays of shaded lights which will dim when the coffin begins its journey.

Before that, though, there will be the faint dribble of a hymn, which is for the most part unsung by the men and only falteringly by the women. The deceased is unknown to the vicar, who in turn is a stranger to the mourners, the only participant on intimate terms with all concerned, the corpse included, being the undertaker. Unsolemn, hygienic and somehow retail, the service is so scant as to be scarcely a ceremony at all, and is not so much simple as inadequate. These clipboard send-offs have no swell to them, no tide, there is no launching for the soul, flung like Excalibur over the dark waters. How few lives now end full-throated to hymns soaring or bells pealing from the tower. How few escape a pinched suburban send-off, the last of a life some half-known relatives strolling thankfully back to the car. Behind the boundary of dead rattling beech careful flower beds shelter from the wind, the pruned stumps of roses protruding from a bed of wood-chips.

My mother's funeral is all this, and her sisters' too; gruesome occasions, shamefaced even and followed by an unconvivial meal. Drink would help but our family has never been good at that, tea the most we ever run to with the best cups put out. Still, Mam's life does have a nice postscript when *en secondes funèbres* she is brought together with my father and her ashes put in his grave.

This takes place in the graveyard in the village where the vicar, the bluff straightforward bearded Mr Dalby, digs the little hole himself and puts together a makeshift service. Consolation is inappropriate as no one is grieving and, the prayers over, we are uncertain what to do. We stand there with the wind threshing the sycamores, wondering if that is all there is and if we can go now.

It ought to be me or my brother who takes charge, but after a moment or two's awkward waiting with wonderful inappropriateness it is my friend Anne, unrelated and now entirely unconnected with the family, who picks up some earth and throws it into the casket, whereupon we all follow suit.

'Well,' I can imagine my mother saying, as she did when excusing some lapse or discounting the gossip, 'well, she's right enough.'

Now we stroll back up to the village where she had come in such despair and anguish of mind twenty-five years before. I still live here with my partner, as the phrase is, who is fonder of the house and the village even than I am. He is thirty years younger than me and what the village makes of this I do not know and now at last I do not care. That, at least, my parents' lives have taught me.

Postscript

The church in our village is not one that Philip Larkin would have thought worth stopping for and I fancy he wouldn't even have bothered to take off his cycle clips. Rebuilt in the early nineteenth century, it's neither frowsty nor much-accoutred but barn it certainly is, a space that on the few occasions I've seen it full never seems so and even a large congregation in full voice sounds thin and inadequate.

I think of this church often these days as it will be where my funeral will doubtless be held and hymn-singing, though I seldom do it nowadays, has always been for me a great pleasure. But not in our village church and I feel sorry for the congregation that has to sing me out.

Nor, I'm afraid, is there much to divert the eye, with few monuments to muse on, no glass to speak of, no screen, just a plainness and lack of ornament that in a small church might be appealing but in a place the size of this seem frigid and bare.

There are, it's true, glimpses through the clear glass of the trees in the churchyard outside, and the churchyard is altogether pleasanter than the church it surrounds. Painted once by John Piper for Osbert Sitwell (his series of paintings of the village now at Renishaw), the churchyard is backed by trees with the beck on one side and a waterfall behind, and it looks over some cottages across the lane and down to the village below. Not a bad place to end up, I think, except that I shan't, as the graveyard is full and burials nowadays are in the overflow cemetery on the other side of the bypass (built *circa* 1970) and en route for the station. To reach this graveyard means walking down to the end of the village and then, since the A65 is the main road to the Lake District and traffic incessant, taking the underpass put in specifically for cows and schoolchildren living south of the village. The tunnel also carries the beck which, if in spate, tends to flood the gate at the other end and so means wet feet.

None of which matters if coming by car (or hearse), though mourners should be prepared for a long wait at the bypass and an unhearselike scoot across when there's a rare break in the traffic. On the left as you go down the road is one of Coultherd's fields, which if it's a weekend will have its quota of caravans and the occasional camper.

The cemetery is small and surrounded by trees,

sycamore mostly and horse chestnut but not the preferred beech. When we first came to the village in 1966 there was still a chapel of rest here, but that has gone, though a patch of red and buff tiles still marks the spot, some of which we bought from the parish and now form our kitchen floor. The only other building is a dilapidated shed in the south-eastern corner which also shelters the water butt.

The graves are in rows, some of them unmarked and very few of them with kerbs and plots, the graveyard largely laid to grass. My father's grave and my mother's ashes are on what is currently the last row on the eastern edge. He died in August 1974 aged seventy-one, and my mother nearly twenty years later when she was ninety-one. His neighbours in death are folks he may have known to say 'Good morning' to, most of the people buried here on those sort of terms, some of them families like Cross and Kay and Nelson who have been in the village for generations.

When I ordered the gravestone for my father I made some effort not to have one of the shiny marble jobs with gilt letters that most people seem to go in for. I wanted it plain, as plain as one of the war graves in France. And so it is, though not looking quite like that, as stained by damp and with too much in the way of lettering and so rather crowded.

On the grave is a kitchen storage jar which we use for flowers, anything more elaborate likely to be stolen. The flowers I periodically put there are from the garden, which Dad would have liked, though in the summer when the grass grows the place is a sea of dog daisies which he would have liked more, the whole graveyard a haven for wild flowers. One in particular grows here and is a favourite of mine, the water avens (*Geum rivale*), which Richard Mabey describes as having 'cup-shaped flowers, flushed with purple, pink and dull orange', which for some reason suggests strawberries though the strawberry flower is white. He also says it's 'a glamorous and secretive species', and in the cemetery it grows round the water butt where I fill the storage jar.

Filling the jar at the water butt reminds me of a similar watering place, a tap and an iron trough in New Wortley Cemetery down Tong Road, where I used to go with my grandmother as a child to tend that unmarked grass-covered tump that was my grandfather's grave. Because it was unmarked I was never certain of its precise location,

'Don't pull your jib, Dad. Smile!'

and finding my way back there from the cistern, both hands gripped round a brimming vase, was never easy. Grandma is a tall woman, but she is likely to be bent down over the grave and invisible behind the gravestones. I dodge in and out among the graves, holding the heavy vase, trying to find a way through this sepulchral maze. I think I am lost and will never find it but then that is what I always think and suddenly, rounding an angel, I come upon Grandma on her knees snipping at the grass with her kitchen scissors.

The anemones she has bought at Sleights, the greengrocer on the corner of Green Lane, are put in the vase and we thread our way out, walking back hand in hand down the main avenue towards the cemetery gates with the battlements of Armley Gaol looming up behind us.

Sometimes as I'm standing by their grave I try and get a picture of my parents, Dad in his waistcoat and shirtsleeves, Mam in her blue coat and shiny straw hat. I even try and say a word or two in prayer, though what and to what I'd find it hard to say.

'Now then' is about all it amounts to. Or 'Very good, very good', which is what old men say when a transaction is completed.

ff

Faber and Faber – a home for writers

Faber and Faber is one of the great independent publishing houses in London. We were established in 1929 by Geoffrey Faber and our first editor was T. S. Eliot. We are proud to publish prize-winning fiction and non-fiction, as well as an unrivalled list of modern poets and playwrights. Among our list of writers we have five Booker Prize winners and eleven Nobel Laureates, and we continue to seek out the most exciting and innovative writers at work today.

www.faber.co.uk – a home for readers

The Faber website is a place where you will find all the latest news on our writers and events. You can listen to podcasts, preview new books, read specially commissioned articles and access reading guides, as well as entering competitions and enjoying a whole range of offers and exclusives. You can also browse the list of Faber Finds, an exciting new project where reader recommendations are helping to bring a wealth of lost classics back into print using the latest on-demand technology.